Re-Engaging
Students for Success

Re-Engaging Students for Success

Planning for the Education Teaching Performance Assessment

Kathleen G. Velsor

ROWMAN & LITTLEFIELD
Lanham • Boulder • New York • London

Published by Rowman & Littlefield
A wholly owned subsidiary of The Rowman & Littlefield Publishing Group, Inc.
4501 Forbes Boulevard, Suite 200, Lanham, Maryland 20706
www.rowman.com

Unit A, Whitacre Mews, 26-34 Stannary Street, London SE11 4AB

British Library Cataloguing in Publication Information Available

Library of Congress Cataloging-in-Publication Data

Velsor, Kathleen, 1947-
  Re-engaging students for success : planning for the education teaching performance
assessment / Kathleen G. Velsor.
      pages cm
  Includes bibliographical references and index.
  ISBN 978-1-4758-1394-4 (hardcover) — ISBN 978-1-4758-1395-1 (pbk.) — ISBN
978-1-4758-1396-8 (e-book) 1. Teachers—Rating of—United States. 2. Teachers—
Training of—United States. 3. Lesson planning—United States. 4. Academic
language—United States. I. Title.
  LB2838.V45 2015
  371.1020973—dc23
                                                                          2015014482

Printed in the United States of America

To all elementary teacher candidates who have the desire to teach.

To my teacher candidates at Old Westbury, my heartfelt thanks for using this methodology to pass the edTPA.

Finally, I dedicate this book to Curtis Velsor, my husband, mentor, and friend. Thank you.

Contents

Foreword

Jessica Spero

This methodology helped me to pass the edTPA. The way I wrote my lesson plans helped my overall scoring. Over the years at Old Westbury, I learned about Bloom's taxonomy, but I never incorporated it into my lesson planning. Dr. Velsor assisted us in adding Bloom's taxonomy to our learning targets and actually writing them out in the lesson plan. This helped the flow of my lessons. I wish I had developed lesson plans like this sooner. It enabled me to go through each target remembering, understanding, applying, analyzing, evaluating, and creating. My video looked rehearsed even though it wasn't, and I was organized and prepared to guide the students through each learning target. This way, I was able to ensure student completion of each target before I moved on to a different one. If my students didn't do quite as well as I had hoped, I could guide them through and make sure they understood before moving on. Also, this way of clearly setting up each learning target helped me when it came to the student assessment part of the edTPA. I was able to create an accurate rubric based off of it. I strongly believe this helped me get points in the assessing tasks because it was clear to the reader what I wanted the students to achieve and how they did that.

I want to stress how important it is to support varied student learning needs. I incorporated many modifications and adaptations for my students with attention deficit hyperactivity disorder, English language learners, limited English proficient students, and gifted students both on my lesson plans and in my write-ups. Students should point out what they did to accommodate at least one child with varied learning needs when they do their write-up in the commentaries on their video. For example, at five minutes and twenty-six seconds, I played the audio version of the story for my students who had trouble reading (after they read it silently), so that they could comprehend the story rather than struggle with unfamiliar words while reading. This is the only category on the edTPA where I received a four on the rubric. For everything else I got all threes.

Acknowledgments

To my colleagues at the State University of New York at the College at Old Westbury: Dr. Jeanne Shimizu, assistant professor of math education, who guided my writing in the math overview. Thank you for your comments and questions during the writing of this manuscript. To Geraldine A. Faivre, adjunct professor and former head of Westbury Friends School, East Woods Lower School, and the Jewish Academy, a thank you for your vision and continual support of this guidebook. Your perspective and encouragement will help future candidates to believe in themselves as they work through the many written prompts. Dr. Stephanie Schneider, assistant professor in elementary literacy and edTPA coordinator, thank you for sharing your ideas and for providing access to the correct nationwide pass rates of the 2014 edition of the edTPA.

To Joseph Fiorita and Elfrida Oni, fall 2014 teacher candidates, many thanks to you for reviewing and sharing your enthusiasm and suggestions. Thanks to Jessica Spero for sharing her exam so that every candidate can access this successful model.

Preface

This guidebook is designed to provide elementary school teaching candidates with an educational methodology to pass the Education Teaching Performance Assessment (hereafter referred to as edTPA). This methodology can be used to plan, implement, and assess student learning during instruction, which is required to pass the edTPA. The design was originally presented in the book *Engaging Students: Using the Unit in Comprehensive Lesson Planning.*[1] The academic language has been modified to correspond with the academic language used in the edTPA, but the concepts remain the same.

Additionally, this method assists elementary teacher candidates in assessing student learning while managing classroom instruction. Candidates who have used this method have been successful in passing the edTPA.

NOTE

1. Beirne, Dianna, and Kathleen Velsor. *Engaging Students: Using the Unit in Comprehensive Lesson Planning.* New York: Rowman & Littlefield Education, 2012.

Introduction

As of spring 2014, New York, Tennessee, Washington, and Wisconsin all require preservice teacher candidates to pass the Education Teaching Performance Assessment (edTPA) to earn initial teaching certification. California, Georgia, Ohio, and Massachusetts are planning to adopt the edTPA as early as 2015, and eighteen other states are considering adopting this policy in the near future.

Pearson reported that 53 percent of candidates in New York State seeking elementary certification passed the edTPA in the spring of 2014.[1] New York State's website reported that 80 percent of the candidates passed.[2] New York State's reported pass rates were obtained from only the students who elected to send their scores to the state after completing the exam. The edTPA is the culmination of twenty-five years of work by professional educators to develop performance-based assessments of teaching quality and effectiveness.[3]

During spring 2014, college students in New York State were overwhelmed by the new requirements. Melissa Howard, a teacher candidate from New Hyde Park, New York, developed an online petition to "indefinitely suspend implementation of edTPA until the flaws have been fixed." When the site shut down in August 2014, six thousand supporters had signed the petition.

Melissa listed a number of complaints, including the inherent difficulties in using videos to assess teaching skills, and questioned the qualifications of the reviewers. She also states: "Further issues that we have with edTPA itself include a lack of clarity in the language used in the edTPA handbook. Because of the vague wording, it is unclear what is expected of us. The language used also contradicts existing educational literature."[4]

In an effort to appease those affected by the new regulations, the New York State Regents agreed to postpone the regulation until the 2015–2016 academic year. New York State Chancellor King agreed to the requirement that teacher candidates take the edTPA, but if they failed, an academic "parachute" allows the candidates to take a paper exam.

So what is the confusion over "vague wording"?

ACADEMIC LANGUAGE

The underlining theory about academic language and learning comes from J. D. Wilhelm, who writes extensively about the power of language. "When we teach a subject of any topic or text within a subject, we must teach the academic vocabulary for dealing with it. Not just the words, but also the linguistic processes and patterns for delivering deeply into and operating upon the content."[5]

A key concept in successfully completing the edTPA is the use of academic language. Academic language is the language used in a particular academic discipline. For the edTPA, the candidate is required to use the academic language of the discipline of education, as well as the disciplines of literacy and math. Thus, the language in the edTPA handbook is confusing for candidates to connect to their course preparation.

Academic language is demonstrated to the evaluator through the use of vocabulary and through syntax. Syntax simply means using the vocabulary correctly in a complete sentence. Academic language can be demonstrated through the candidate's spoken responses during the video clip lesson segment and through the candidate's written responses. Academic language is also demonstrated through students' voices during the video lesson segment and through student work samples.

For example, a comprehension question such as "What is the main idea of the paragraph? Please include place and setting in your response," uses the academic language of literature. The main idea, place, and setting are terms used to analyze literature. These vocabulary words can be found in the common core standards and the literacy text. This will be discussed in more detail throughout this book.

Educators are masters of creating new language patterns; this is the power behind the edTPA. Each section of this guidebook highlights the academic language that enhances the elementary teacher candidates' presentations.

This book is presented in six chapters with a glossary of academic language and two appendixes to assist the candidate in the interpretation of the meaning of each prompt. Written and verbal responses can be enhanced with the use of academic language. The glossary is designed to assist the candidate in using academic language in an appropriate way.

CHAPTER 1: INSTRUCTIONAL PLANNING

In chapter 1, the academic language is focused on the candidates' responses to prompts about the school district to which they have been assigned. This chapter addresses questions on the edTPA that involve the school where the candidate is teaching, the class featured in this assessment, and the students in the class featured in this assessment. The candidates' use of academic language in regard to core instruction in literacy and math and their work with students whose primary language is not English is addressed.

CHAPTER 2: INSTRUCTIONAL PLANNING FOR THE edTPA; CHAPTER 3: LESSON PLANNING; AND CHAPTER 4: UNIT PLANNING

In chapters 2, 3, and 4, the candidate is expected to use educational language geared to the edTPA and the discipline language of literacy and math. The discipline's academic language is generated from the common core standards and from the text. This will be explained using actual lesson plans.

CHAPTER 5: ASSESSMENT

In chapter 5, assessment unites the academic language of education with the academic language of literacy and math. The candidate is required to discuss the assessment of the student work samples using formative and summative assessment of academic language to document student learning. This data is then used to generate the second and third lesson in the unit. This addition was added to the 2014 exam.

CHAPTER 6: edTPA RESPONSE BY JESSICA SPERO

Chapter 6 is an actual response to the spring 2014 exam by Jessica Spero, who demonstrated the use of academic language in education, literacy, and math.

THINGS TO REMEMBER

- Education Teaching Performance Assessment is referred to as edTPA.
- California, Georgia, Ohio, and Massachusetts are planning to adopt the edTPA as early as 2015.
- Melissa Howard states: "Further issues that we have with edTPA itself include a lack of clarity in the language used in the edTPA handbook. Because of the vague wording, it is unclear what is expected of us."
- A key concept in successfully completing the edTPA is the use of academic language.
- Academic language is the language used in a particular academic discipline.
- Academic language is demonstrated to the evaluator through the use of vocabulary and syntax.
- Syntax simply means using the vocabulary correctly in a complete sentence.

NOTES

1. Education report.net. This is a private site that can be accessed only with a pass code.
2. New York State Education Department, nysed.gov/higheredcert.
3. Stanford Center for Assessment and Equity, *edTPA Elementary Education Assessment Handbook*, 2013.
4. Melissa Howard, "Indefinitely Suspend Implementation of edTPA until the Flaws Have Been Fixed," www.change.org/p/new-york-state-house-indefinitely-suspend-implementation-of-edtpa-until-the-flaws-have-been-fixed.
5. Wilhelm, J. D. "Imagining a New Kind of Self: Academic Language Identity, and Content Area Learning." National Council of Teachers of English, *Voices from the Middle*, 15nlp4(2007): 44–45.

1

Instructional Planning

SETTING THE STAGE FOR
PLANNING THE edTPA LEARNING SEGMENTS

As we begin our journey to student teaching, it is important to remember that the classroom is a microcosm of the larger community that it serves. With this in mind, planning for the edTPA can begin as soon as the candidate receives notification of a placement. The edTPA asks the candidate to describe the nature of the school district where the instruction is taking place. Most school districts have a website. The website can provide the candidate with directions to the school, a contact number, the school calendar, and other pertinent information about the district.

WHAT CAN CANDIDATES
DO BEFORE STUDENT TEACHING BEGINS?

For the purpose of this book, we feature a real school district within the geographic suburban vicinity of New York City. On the district website, the school mission reads: "to support students' academic, social, and moral growth." There are three elementary schools: one kindergarten center and two primary schools for first and second grade and two schools for third, fourth, and fifth graders. The school website lists news items and information about filing for the free lunch program.

On the school district website under the tab for English language learners (ELL), three programs are listed: traditional bilingual classes for prekindergarten through third grade, English as a second language for kindergarten through twelfth grade, and a dual-language program for kindergarten through fifth grade.

WHAT CAN CANDIDATES DO TO PREPARE AFTER REVIEWING THE DISTRICT WEBSITE?

The candidate should begin reviewing current policies that support programs for students whose second language is English. For example, an outgrowth of the Individuals with Disabilities Act (IDEA), Public Law 108-446 (U.S. Department of Education, 2006) is for the development of reading programs known as response to intervention (RTI). School districts are responsible for designing a multi-tier approach to reading assessments for all students in general and special education.[1]

As a result of this legislation, each teacher is required to complete an individual reading assessment (IRA) for each of their students. Working with teachers across grade levels and with reading specialists, each school is responsible for designing a systematic way to respond to intervention for reading support and for the continual improvement for all students. The RTI is a process of rating how each student is performing in relation to a given set of standards set by the International Reading Association (IRA).

The RTI in each school district must have a reading program that identifies four different levels derived from International Reading Association criteria and the student population. The reading levels and tiers I, II, and III provide the academic language that the candidate is expected to use when responding to prompts in the edTPA.

The first is referred to as core instruction. Tier I, tier II, and tier III instruction is for students who range from almost at grade level to those students who have an individual reading program.

The core instruction is the classroom instruction for all students. Core instruction is broken into learning segments. Each learning segment is part of a larger unit discussed in chapter 3. The lessons are referred to as the learning segment. In the literacy and math learning segments, the candidate is asked to design learning tasks for each lesson in the learning segment.

Tasks are assessments used during instruction so that the candidate can first identify tier I students who show some difficulty with a given learning segment. These students are typically given a "mini-lesson" or a different strategy to complete the given task. This is completed during the classroom lesson and is discussed further in chapter 3.

Tier II students need a separate learning segment; this is referred to as a reengagement lesson. This lesson can be in a small or large group session. The reengagement lesson is derived from the summative assessment of the learning segment. The candidate can complete an analysis of the task data after the learning segment is completed. This lesson is called a reengagement lesson in the edTPA and is discussed in chapter 5.

Tier III students are students who need special intervention. For the purpose of the edTPA, these students have been identified as such by the classroom teacher and thus have an individual educational program (IEP). The IEP gives specific guidelines for assisting these students in the classroom. This is discussed in chapter 2.

Literacy development is the process of learning to read, write, speak, and listen. It may also include the process of looking at graphics and visual media.[2] In *Literacy Assessment: Helping Teachers Plan Instruction*, Cooper and Kiger cite five stages of literacy development. These stages remain the same for all students. These concepts are essential for reviewing reading levels in the candidates' classrooms and can be used to describe the reading levels of their students. Using the correct academic language enhances the candidates' responses. These terms include:

- Early emergent literacy. This usually develops before kindergarten and forms the foundation for understanding oral language and being curious about print. Most second language learners have surpassed this stage in their first language.
- Emergent literacy. This stage usually develops in preschool and kindergarten. Students learn about oral sounds and letter recognition. They are using more standard language patterns.
- Beginning reading and writing. This stage develops when students begin to read and write in a more conventional way as their language skills develop. They begin to understand the meaning of words as their fluency increases.

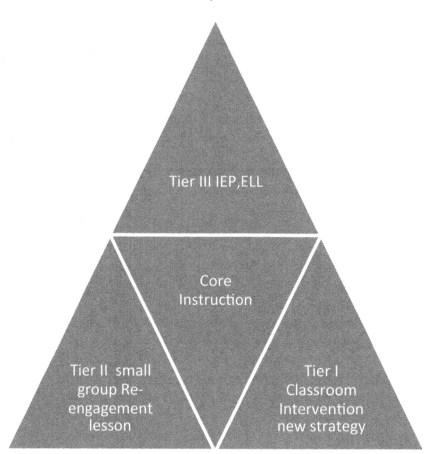

Figure 1.1.   Four Levels of Instruction

- Almost fluent reading and writing. In this stage, children can read si-lently and write more, and they have more oral language skills and an expanded vocabulary. For most students this begins in second grade.
- Fluent reading and writing. This stage occurs when children use reading, writing, and oral language skills for a variety of purposes. This stage begins in fourth grade and continues to develop throughout the rest of their lives.[3]

Literacy is a continual and ongoing process. Jean Piaget held tight to the notion that various factors can accelerate or slow down a child's develop-ment. Environment and heredity play a significant role on a child's academic

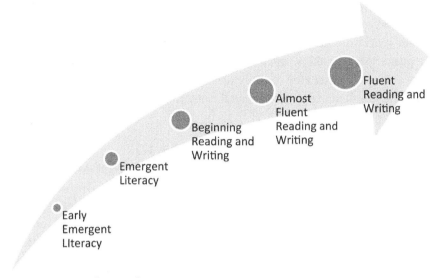

Fluent
Reading and
Writing

Almost
Fluent
Reading and
Writing

Beginning
Reading and
Writing

Emergent
Literacy

Early
Emergent
LIteracy

Figure 1.2. Reading Levels

experiences. Language develops from our experience with people, print, and media. As children assimilate their experiences and accommodate information from multiple sources, they develop language. Literacy is demonstrated through their ability to read, write, speak about, and listen to others.[4]

HOW CAN CANDIDATES IDENTIFY THE NEEDS OF STUDENTS IN THEIR CLASSROOMS?

Candidates beginning student teaching in the fall may need to rely on assessment information in literacy and math provided by the school's principal. Teachers generally are given assessment data from the previous year. This data may not be current, but it is a starting point. Within the first five or six weeks of the school year, teachers are required to complete an individual reading assessment (IRA) to assess each of their students' reading levels.

The key to making assessment-based literacy models is derived from working with colleagues together as a team for the improvement of each student. In a diverse classroom, teachers work with a wide variety of individuals who comprise the class. Besides English language learners coming from a variety of cultural backgrounds, there are individuals with emotional and academic challenges. Despite the differences, the assessment questions remain the same. Where are these students in terms of their listening skills, their oral language speaking skills, and their reading and writing in English? What are they able to do next? How do they feel about themselves? How can you arrange the instructional materials and the environment to help them?[5]

WHY IS IT IMPORTANT TO
ADDRESS THE STUDENTS IN THE CLASSROOM?

The first section of the edTPA is referred to as the "context for learning." The question or prompt that the candidate is asked to respond to focuses on the students in the candidate's classroom. If the school district offers three different approaches to teaching English, it would be prudent for the candidate to research the expectations for teaching in a classroom with a diverse language population.

This school district identified three programs: traditional bilingual classes for prekindergarten through third grade, English as a second language for kindergarten through twelfth grade, and a dual-language program for kindergarten through fifth grade. What is the difference?

English language learners (ELL), in a traditional bilingual class for prekindergarten through third grade and dual-language programs for kindergarten through fifth grade, means that students receive instruction in their native languages and in English until they reach the exit criterion on the New York State English as a Second Language Achievement Test (NYSESLAT). The program goals provide students with native language support until they are ready to be mainstreamed into English-only classes. They support multicultural awareness and appreciation while providing quality instruction in two languages, enabling students to demonstrate mastery in all core subjects using their native languages. English is learned along with other subjects, allowing students to remain on grade level academically while learning English. These students are identified as tier III students.

The dual-language (DL) program invites English-speaking students to speak and write in Spanish as a second language simultaneously. The school district also encourages all ELL parents to learn English at the school so that they can become more active participants in their children's education.[6]

Most states rely on the ACCESS (Assessing Comprehension and Communication in English for English Language Learners) test for ELL student assessments. The ACCESS test assesses the four domains of literacy in English language acquisition: listening, speaking, reading, and writing. Students receive a score in each domain: level 1 entering; level 2 beginning; level 3 developing; level 4 expanding; level 5 bridging; and level 6 reaching. This test exceeds the requirements set by the No Child Left Behind (NCLB) Act of 2001 and is used to measure growth while setting criterion for instruction.[7]

Either of these tests—New York State English as a Second Language Achievement Test (NYSESLAT) or Assessing Comprehension and Communication in English for English Language Learners (ACCESS)—can be used to identify what reading level the students have achieved. If the test results are not available for the candidate to use, at least the candidate knows the name of the tests and can refer to them in the commentary about the classroom setting. When responding to the prompt question on the edTPA, the candidate can mention this as a reference.

Inclusion programs involve students who are identified as exceptional and may be referred to as tier II or tier III students depending on their reading levels. Most classrooms have students who have been classified, and thus a typical classroom may include students with learning disabilities, attention deficit disorder (ADD) or attention deficit hyperactivity disorder (ADHD), and students with some degree of autism. Other students may be identified as gifted and talented. This does not change the expectations for literacy or math development. A diverse classroom is a strong classroom, and it provides the candidate many opportunities to create strategies for these students to succeed.

HOW DOES THIS RELATE TO THE edTPA?

The first question that needs to be addressed before instructional planning can begin is: who are the students in this classroom? The cooperating teacher can provide the candidate with background of the students in the class. Included in the interview should be: the total number of students, the number of students of each gender, the ages of the students, and their reading levels, which can be summarized by category, by number of ELL students, and by number of students identified with special needs and a brief description of their IEPs.

The cooperating teacher can also give the candidate a list of ELL students' first languages and any written reports about students with special needs. When the candidate selects a unit of study to teach, the candidate notes the modifications or adaptations needed for these students. This is discussed further in chapter 3 and in chapter 6.

If the IEP for individual students requires assistance from an aide and the aide is in the classroom, the candidate needs to mention the strategy used to assist each student. This will be discussed under "instructional strategies and adaptations and modification" in the lesson plan in chapter 3. Planning helps the candidate to answer these questions and thus helps to design the instruction.

WHAT CAN THE CANDIDATE DO IF NO ASSESSMENTS ARE AVAILABLE?

Here are some helpful ideas for assessing student learning when test scores are not available.

Create Literacy and Math Tasks Checklists

When planning instruction, it is important to know how the students in the class perform on certain tasks in literacy and in math. Take the current learning segments in both literacy and math that the cooperating teacher is teaching. Review the list of tasks identified in the teachers' manuals or in the teachers' lesson plans.

Make a chart. Identify five tasks in literacy segments and five tasks in the math segments that the students must accomplish in order to move on to the next learning segment. List the tasks on the left side and place the students' names across the top. This simple assessment chart gives the candidate information about each student while helping to learn the students' names. Make a key: X+ equals mastery, X− means that they may need another lesson to master the task, and O means that they have not demonstrated knowledge of the task. As the cooperating teacher models how to teach in the classroom, the candidate completes the checklist.

Now the candidate has baseline data to be used when planning the unit in literacy and math. In this example (figure 1.3), what percentage of the

Math LS 1	Jessica A	Julio B	Robert C	Jan D	Debby E
Task 1	X+	X	X	X	X
Task 2	X-	X+	X	X	X
Task 3	O	O	O	X	O
Task 4	X	X-	X	X	X
Task 5	X	X	X	X	O

Figure 1.3.   **Learning Segment Checklist for Math Learning Segment 1**

students needs another lesson in task 3? There are five students in all, and four did not master the task; that is, 4 divided by 5 equals .8, or 80 percent of the students need another lesson to complete the task. When the candidate records the data after the lesson is completed to use for the next tier II instruction, the edTPA refers to this as a reengagement lesson. This is discussed in chapter 5.

A code could be used to identify diverse learners on the checklist. If the candidate noticed that a particular student is not participating and is an ELL student, the candidate may want to note this in the section devoted to students in the classroom featured in the assessment. This also assists the candidate in planning and including connections to the students' lives in relationship to the lesson. By keeping a running record of each student's progress, the candidate can use this information to assist in the planning stage. This is discussed in chapter 3.

Student Conferences

Teachers often use student conferences to talk about student work and progress. Candidates can use conference time to discuss student work as a way of introducing themselves to the students. Spend some time asking about student interests. The candidate can use a picture book or magazine to focus the discussion. Questions about how the student uses his free time can be helpful. Attitudes about schoolwork and her feelings about herself in school (self-concept) can be informative. Short interviews can help the candidate to make connections to students' lives. Make sure to take notes.[8]

SELF-REFLECTION

After each lesson, ask the students to write what they have learned. Sometimes these are referred to as "exit slips." The candidate can ask each student to write their name on a piece of paper and respond to the question, "what did I learn in this lesson?" Candidates can use this strategy when the cooperating teacher is teaching and especially when the candidate has finished teaching a learning segment.

The student responses provide summative data for the next lesson. The exit slip can also be used in the edTPA to demonstrate the ongoing assessment. The candidate can use the information to determine the percentage of students who used the vocabulary and discussed the concept, as well as the percentage of students who need more instruction for the reengagement lesson. When students are asked to respond to their own learning, they become more engaged in the learning process. The expectation changes and the learner becomes more responsible, helping to create a pattern for teaching and learning in the classroom.[9]

THINGS TO REMEMBER

- Every school district has a website that provides demographics of the district, current news articles, and unique programs offered in the district. Classrooms are microcosms of the larger population in the school district. *Piece of what that community is*
- The edTPA uses the term tasks for literacy learning segments and math learning segments.
- Every school district has a response to intervention (RTI) program. Instruction begins with the core instruction. Tier I students need a mini-lesson or a different strategy to complete the learning task; tier II students need a reengagement lesson to complete the learning task; and tier III students need extra assistance to complete the learning task.
- Literacy development is the process of learning to read, write, speak, and listen. The five stages of literacy development are: early emergent literacy, emergent literacy, beginning reading and writing, almost fluent reading and writing, and fluent reading and writing.

- Identify students comprising the classroom: exceptional learners, English language learners (ELL), students with attention deficit disorder (ADD), attention deficit hyperactivity disorder (ADHD), and autism, as well as their individual educational plans (IEPs).
- Helpful hints to assess student needs include designing a class checklist for literacy and math skills, scheduling individual student conferences, and using self-reflection and exit slips in the classroom.

NOTES

1. Fuchs, D., L. S. Fuchs, and S. Vaughn, ed. *Response to Intervention: A Framework for Reading Educators*. Newark, DE: International Reading Association, 2008. 6.

2. Cooper, David J., and Nancy D. Kiger. *Literacy Assessment: Helping Teachers Plan Instruction*. 4th ed. Belmont, CA: Wadsworth Cengage Learning, 2011. 9.

3. Ibid., 10.

4. Wadsworth, Barry J. *Piaget's Theory of Cognitive and Affective Development: Foundations of Constructivism*. 5th ed. White Plains, NY: Longman Publishers, 1971. 57–60.

5. Cooper and Kiger, *Literacy Assessment: Helping Teachers Plan Instruction*, 9.

6. Hamayan, Else, Fred Genesee, and Nancy Cloud. *Dual Language Instruction for Teachers and Administrators from A–Z*. Portsmouth, NH: Heinemann, 2004. 2.

7. WiDA, www.wida.us/assessment/ACCESS/index.aspx.

8. Cooper and Kiger, *Literacy Assessment: Helping Teachers Plan Instruction*, 10.

9. Tomlinson, Carol Ann, and Jay McTighe. *Integrating Differentiated Instruction Understanding by Design*. Alexandria, VA: Association for Supervision and Curriculum Development, 2006. 21.

2

Instructional Planning for the edTPA

With the adoption of the common core standards, the approach to the classroom curriculum has been changed. Teachers are now approaching literacy and math instruction through standardized units of study in the elementary school curriculum. The cooperating teacher will introduce the candidate to the required text where the units have already been identified. School district administrators adopt texts, and in most cases classroom teachers have attended in-service workshops to ensure that the text is used in a meaningful way.

WHAT REQUIREMENTS OR EXPECTATIONS MIGHT AFFECT PLANNING INSTRUCTION?

Each text series also has a teachers' edition. The teachers' edition identifies the standard and explains the nature of the unit, the sequence of the learning segments, and the expected student outcomes. In some cases the text provides worksheets for students, citing sample responses. The candidate must identify the text used and discuss how it is being implemented in the classroom—this discussion is featured in the assessment section of the exam. If there is no text featured, this needs to be mentioned by the candidate. Telling the evaluator about the materials used helps the evaluator to better understand the nature of instruction in the candidate's school.

WHAT IS REQUIRED FOR THE edTPA?

The cooperating teacher assigns the candidate a unit. According to the edTPA, the candidate needs to design a learning segment in a learning sequence consisting of three to five lessons. The candidate writes three lesson plans for each learning segment in response to the needs of the students as discussed in chapter 1. The lesson plan should be designed to continually assess student learning. This can be accomplished by establishing learning tasks.

What Is a Learning Task?

Learning tasks are well-defined learning outcomes that the candidate writes into the lesson plan. Tasks are used as benchmarks throughout the learning segments. Tasks are sequential. The students must master the first task in order to move to the second task. Rubrics are used to measure the success of the students as they complete each task in the lesson.[1]

The candidate is asked to describe the students used in the assessment. This prompt is to assist the evaluator in understanding the needs of the students who present during the learning segment. The candidate selects one literacy learning segment to videotape.

In the school district outlined in chapter 1, a third grade classroom consists of twenty-one children: thirteen girls and eight boys. Three students have individual education plans (IEPs), one student has attention deficit hyperactivity disorder (ADHD), and four students are English language learners (ELL). The candidate is asked to complete a chart to describe the needed supports, adaptations, and modifications that will affect the literacy lesson.

The candidate can work with the cooperating teacher to find the answers to these learning modifications. In chapter 6, the edTPA candidate Jessica Spero completed an extensive response to this question.

IEP/504 Plans Classification/Needs	Number of Students	Supports, Accommodations, Modifications, Pertinent IEP Goals

Figure 2.1. Adaptations and Modifications

Many classrooms have students who have been identified with ADHD. Under the column "supports, accommodations, modifications, pertinent IEP goals," the candidate in chapter 6 explained that

> the student sits with a good role model, is allowed extra time to complete independent tasks. The student is paired with another student who explains written instructions. The partner and aid seek to involve student in the lesson. The student is given guided instruction when answering a question. The student is provided with short breaks between assignments and is frequently complimented for positive behavior with work prompts. The student is encouraged to read small amounts at a time.

The different reading levels of the students in the class need to be identified. For example, if there are students who are not fluent readers, the candidate can report: "The reading teacher works with these students during English language arts (ELA) block. The reading teacher uses audio texts for these students to hear fluent reading, which helps with comprehension. The reading teacher also assists them while they are working independently."

There are a number of students for whom English is not their first language. The ELL students are assisted with the use of audio texts. The ELL students are given targeted, guided reading, guided questioning, and cooperative learning groups with their peers. The ELL students are taught new vocabulary in context of sentences to facilitate comprehension. Informal assessments allow room for oral assessments. Language is communicated through the use of actions and gestures to explain unfamiliar words.

Does the Candidate Need to Write Four Different Lesson Plans for This Class for the edTPA?

No.

In the "No Child Left Behind" classroom, all students will learn. All students need to complete each task. Some may need assistance. This can be accomplished using different strategies as described in the "supports, accommodations" section. Everyone needs to meet the task.

WRITING TASKS: USING BLOOM'S TAXONOMY AS YOUR GUIDE

In 1948 Benjamin Bloom and a group of educators designed a taxonomy for higher order thinking skills. The taxonomy originally identified three domains: cognitive, affective, and psychomotor.[2] In 2001 the cognitive domain was reassessed by Lori Anderson and David Krathwohl and designed to better align with the needs of students in today's classrooms.

These changes provide new terms to the original six levels of the cognitive domain. The table revised by Anderson and Krathwohl lists the lowest cognitive level, (1) remembering, to the highest cognitive level, (6) creating. Learners must obtain each level before moving to the next level. Therefore learners can apply knowledge of a subject only after they have remembered and explained the new knowledge. Thus, for the student to create something such as a poem or a picture, the candidate needs to design a task for six different levels.

Anderson and Krathwohl's revised cognitive [thinking] levels:

1. *Remembering*: retrieving, recognizing, and recalling relevant knowledge from long-term memory.
2. *Understanding*: constructing meaning from oral, written, and graphic messages through interpreting, exemplifying, classifying, summarizing, inferring, comparing, and explaining.
3. *Applying*: carrying out or using a procedure through executing or implementation.
4. *Analyzing*: breaking down material into constituent parts; determining how parts relate to one another and to an overall structure or purpose through differentiating, organizing, and attributing.
5. *Evaluating*: making judgments based on criteria and standards through checking and critique.
6. *Creating*: putting elements together to form a coherent or functional whole; reorganizing elements into a new pattern or structure through generating, planning, and producing.

Read the list again. This time look for verbs. Each level acts as a task to be completed in the lesson plan. Each task provides assessment information. This data can be used for the assessment of student learning for the edTPA. The candidate is required to have an assessment plan; this will be discussed in chapter 5.

Figure 2.2.   Take Another Look at the Six Levels of Cognitive Domains

How Do Learning Tasks Differ from Learning Objectives?

The learning objective is what students accomplish at the end of the lesson. The learning objective is derived from the common core standards or state standards, depending upon where the candidate is student teaching. Like the response to intervention, the standards hold the framework for instruction. The learning tasks are the steps necessary to complete the learning objective, which is derived from the standards. The standards were developed to ensure that students—regardless of geographic location or economic opportunity—receive an equal education. Therefore all instruction is designed to assist the learner in accomplishing a task, which is a stepping-stone to accomplishing the standard.

Often candidates include the word "understand" in an objective ("students will understand . . ."). However, it is very difficult to measure understanding, which is cognitive level. Use words that describe understanding, such as "students will verbally explain the meaning of the five vocabulary words to their partners." The candidate needs to ask the question, "what do I want my students to produce throughout the lesson?" Using the appropriate Bloom terminology makes the outcome measureable.[3]

How Can the Candidate Apply This Concept for a Third Grade Math Lesson?

For the purpose of explaining how to use the revised Bloom's taxonomy concepts, consider a math lesson in geometry. All lessons are tied to the common core standards in the school district we chose for our model. These are generally listed in the textbook; if not, they can be found easily on the Internet:

> Math common core standard 3G1: Reason with shapes and their attributes. Understand that shapes in different categories (e.g., rhombuses, rectangles, and others) may share the attributes (e.g., having four sides) and that the shared attributes can define a larger category (e.g., quadrilaterals). Recognize rhombuses, rectangles, and squares as examples of parallelograms, and draw examples of quadrilaterals that do not belong to any of these categories.[4]

If, for example, the candidate is asked to design a lesson that meets the third grade math standard in geometry, this is how she might proceed. The learning tasks for this third grade math lesson are derived from Bloom's revised list. The first task is to see if the students remember (list) the different categories. The second task is to see if the students understand (explain) the attributes. The third task is to see if the students could apply this information by drawing the shapes.

How is the candidate going to know that the students have satisfied the standard? What are the students going to do to let the candidate know that they understand the concept? Figure 2.3 organizes the skills and provides the candidate with a list of verbs and products that can become the task for each level in a lesson.

The first learning task for math and for literacy in every lesson is remembering. Refer to figure 2.3.[5] The verbs listed for "remembering" are: list, memorize, review, define, name, match, retrieve, recognize, and recall. In this lesson in third grade math, what do the students need to remember? Categories? How are the students going to demonstrate that they remember the six types of quadrilaterals?

Bloom's Higher Order Thinking Skills	Verbs	Products
Remembering: students express and recall information	list, memorize, review, define, name, match, retrieve, recognize, recall	label, list, definition, test, reproduction, recitation, tape
Understanding: students construct meaning from oral, graphic, or written messages	explain, summarize, generalize, interpret, infer, paraphrase, classify	report, illustration, matching chart, demonstration, dramatization
Applying: students use new information across contexts, executing and implementing a procedure	apply, construct, demonstrate, solve, show, translate, illustrate	diagram, model, report, lesson, photograph, collection, map, puzzle, diary
Analyzing: students break material into constituent parts, determining how the parts relate to the whole	analyze, distinguish, differentiate, classify, contrast, compare, order	diagram, questionnaire, graph, outline, survey, report, chart, conclusion
Evaluating: students make judgments based on criteria and standards through checking and critique	integrate, compose, formulate, modify, hypothesize, create, invent	plan, formulate, invention, design, poem, solution, art media/prediction story, advertisement
Creating: students put elements together into a coherent, functional whole or reorganize into a new pattern or structure	judge, decide, evaluate, verify, criticize, defend, select, justify, assess	editorial, debate, scale, verdict, value, recommendation, conclusion, report, opinion

Figure 2.3.   Bloom's Higher Order Thinking Skills
Source: Anderson and Krathwohl (2001, 67–68).

Depending on which lesson in the unit is being taught, the students could demonstrate they remember in different ways. The edTPA requires that the candidate sequence three to five lessons for a unit in math. The standard requires that the students know six types of quadrilaterals.

The first lesson would be designed to introduce the unit and provide basic information about lines. The standards are designed to be accumulative from kindergarten through twelfth grade. Theoretically, the students are introduced to geometry in kindergarten, first, and second grades.

The unit design needs to begin with an assessment of previous student learning; this is discussed in the unit design in chapter 3.

Learning segment lesson 1 focuses on the use of learning objectives and tasks for the purpose of setting up an ongoing assessment system. The learning objective needs to reflect a specific outcome that students produce at the end of the lesson.[6] This is the fourth lesson in the unit; unit planning is discussed in chapter 4. The learning objective is for students to draw four parallelograms and label three characteristics. The learning tasks are:

Remembering—Task: List four shapes that could be called parallelograms (e.g., square, rectangle, parallelogram, rhombus). After each student has listed four shapes, the candidate can ask for an explanation of why each shape is a parallelogram.

Understanding—Task: Summarize in your own words three characteristics of a parallelogram (e.g., four-sided shape where opposite sides are parallel and opposite angles are equal).

Applying—Task: Draw four parallelogram shapes and label each of the three characteristics.

Each task requires an assessment rubric to track the students' progress.

Figure 2.4 is an example of the rubric used to assess each student's progress to obtain the math standard 3G1. Acceptable identifies what the students have completed that is close to a completed task. Unacceptable defines what performance requires extra help. This could be a new strategy or another lesson. If the candidate reviews the data and finds that another lesson is needed for a group of students in tier II, this is referred to as a reengagement lesson in the edTPA.

Does Each Task Have to Be Completed to Succeed?

Each task needs to be completed during the instructional lesson. After the candidate begins the learning segment, the first assessment determines if the

Math Standard 3G1	Unacceptable 1 Tier 3	Acceptable 2 Tier 2	Target 3 Tier 1	Score
Remembering	List two or fewer shapes that could be called parallelograms	List three shapes that could be called parallelograms	List four shapes that could be called parallelograms	
Understanding	Summarize two or fewer characteristics of parallelograms	Summarize three characteristics of parallelograms	Summarize in your own words three characteristics of parallelograms	
Applying	Draw two or fewer parallelogram shapes and label two or fewer characteristics	Draw three parallelogram shapes and label three characteristics	Draw four parallelogram shapes and label each shape with four characteristics	

Figure 2.4.   Instructional Assessment Rubric Math Standard 3G1

students remember four shapes that could be called parallelograms. Depending on the prior knowledge of the students and what they remember from the first three lessons in the learning segment, this could be an introduction or a main point in the instruction.

For example, the candidate can start the lesson with a question: "can anyone tell me what a parallelogram is?" Sixteen hands go up and the students verbally explain shapes that are parallelograms. The candidate quickly draws them on the smartboard, checking for response from the five who did not raise their hands, and finds that the students can generally respond to the question. The candidate moves on to the next task, saying, "please take out your math notebooks and write by yourself three characteristics of a parallelogram."

The candidate made an assessment that the students knew four shapes that were parallelograms. The task was met through discussion. The next task will be demonstrated through writing. If the candidate sees that some students are having difficulty defining the terms, the candidate can redirect the tier I learning to accommodate the learners. This may mean grouping students who can explain the characteristics. It may mean redirecting the students to a poster on the wall that has the characteristics of shapes and asking them to find four that may apply to the parallelograms.

It could be that the students cannot answer the question, at which point the candidate redirects the students, explaining the characteristics of the rectangle and asking another student to explain the characteristics of a square. Each or all of these actions can be used in the edTPA as evidence of formative assessments. This is discussed further in chapter 5.

In each scenario, the candidate is making an assessment of student learning. These are both formative assessments completed in an informal way. This is an important key idea. Formative assessments are assessments that candidates use to make informed decisions about student learning in the classroom. Informal means that the candidate is not necessarily using a student work sample to make the assessment. The candidate is listening to student responses and is making a decision to move ahead with the lesson. This is referred to as procedural fluency and is discussed further in chapter 5. The key idea is that there is a task to complete before moving on. The assessment is embedded in the lesson.

Revisiting the Math Lesson

Revisiting this lesson, the candidate this time asks: "can anyone tell me what a parallelogram is?" The students look at the candidate with blank faces, and one student raises his hand and tells the class that he went to the zoo over the weekend and saw two of them in the reptile tank. The candidate now knows that she needs to redirect the lesson using a different strategy. This may take ten minutes. The candidate decides to use a pop-up math video on the smartboard that illustrates the properties of the shapes.[7]

Again the candidate has used an informal formative assessment to move the lesson forward. Was one approach better than the other? No. In each example, the candidate was responsive to the learners in the classroom and can justify the direction and instructional methods needed to go forward with the

Figure 2.5.   Revisiting the Math Lesson

learning segment. In both cases, the candidate was working with three identi-fied tasks, each task a benchmark to move to the next benchmark.

How Would the Candidate Select Tasks for a Lesson in a Literacy Unit on Poetry?

The cooperating teacher in a fourth grade has asked the candidate to develop a lesson in the unit on poetry. The previous lesson was on haikus. Let's say that it is March and the teacher is asking the candidate to develop a learn-ing segment on limericks for St. Patrick's Day. Where should the candidate begin?

The candidate needs to reference the standard for poetry. If the text does not provide the standard for poetry, it can be found online under the common core standards for English language arts grade four under literature, specifi-cally under the standard for "craft and structure":

> CCSSELA Literacy RL45: Explain major differences between poems, drama, and prose, and refer to the structural elements of poems (e.g., verse, rhythm, meter) and drama (e.g., cast of characters, settings, descriptions, dialogue stage directions) when writing or speaking about a text.[8]

This standard is broad. For our purposes, this is a lesson in a unit on poetry. This lesson is the second in the learning segment in the unit on poetry. This learning segment is about limericks, and the focus is on verse, rhythm, and meter. The next step is to find poems on the Bloom's Higher Order Thinking Skills (figure 2.3).

Poetry falls in the category "evaluating." What does this mean? The lesson needs to have tasks in five cognitive domains: remembering, understanding, application, analysis, and evaluating. Why? Writing poems requires the can-didate to confirm that the students complete the needed tasks.

What does the candidate need to remember?

Standard RL45 requires that the students learn poetry with an emphasis on verse, rhythm, and meter. The learner needs to remember the academic lan-guage used: verse, rhythm, and meter. The learner needs to remember the verse in a limerick is a specific meter and rhyming sequence. The learner needs to explain the academic language as it relates to limericks. The learner needs to apply this to an example of a limerick. The learner needs to analyze how rhyming is applied to a limerick. The learner needs to remember what characteristics are used in limericks. The learner can then write a limerick and check against the criteria of verse, rhythm, and meter.

There are six identified tasks that the students need to complete to master this section of the standard and to write a limerick:

Remembering—Task: List three terms used in poetry.
Remembering—Task: List three characteristics of a limerick (e.g., verse, rhythm, and meter).
Understanding—Task: Explain the rhythmic pattern of a limerick.
Applying—Task: Listen to a limerick and explain three characteristics (e.g., why it is silly, rhythm, and meter).
Analyzing—Task: Diagram a limerick to demonstrate rhythm and meter.
Evaluating—Task: Write a limerick.

Standard CCSSELA RL45	Unacceptable	Acceptable	Target	Score
Remembering			List three terms used in poetry	
Remembering			List three characteristics of limericks (verse, rhythm, and meter)	
Understanding			Explain the rhythmic pattern of a limerick	
Applying			Listen to a limerick and explain three characteristics (e.g., why it is silly, rhythm, and meter)	
Analyzing			Diagram a limerick to demonstrate rhythm and meter	
Evaluating			Write a limerick	

Figure 2.6.   Instructional Assessment Rubric Limericks

Tasks Guide the Instruction in the Literacy Learning Segment

By now it must be apparent that tasks guide the learning segment. The tasks set the benchmarks for the learner to obtain. If the candidate notes that the students are obtaining the task, then the candidate knows that the material is making sense. Likewise, if the students are not obtaining the task, it is not making sense to the learners for whatever reason. When the candidate needs to redirect the lesson based on whether the students are obtaining the task, the candidate can identify the problem based on the completed and incompleted tasks.

For example, if in the poetry lesson the students remember the definition of rhythm and meter but cannot apply the meter of the limerick, then the candidate must change the way he presented the material. Simply tell fourth graders to write a limerick using this method: The first, second, and fifth lines rhyme and have the same number of syllables (meter), typically eight or nine. The third and fourth lines rhyme and have the same number of syllables (meter), typically five or six. Limericks usually start with "There once was a . . ." or "There was a . . ."

Some fourth graders may quickly pick up the concept, but some may not. Counting out the syllables and emphasizing the beat by tapping on a table is a strategy to assist the students in explaining how meter and rhyme play a role in a limerick.

Use the Academic Language of the Standards with Students

In both scenarios, the candidate needs to remember to use the academic language of the standard in the tasks. The edTPA requires that the learners use the academic language correctly. In other words, it is not sufficient to write "rhyme," "meter," and "verse" in the tasks to assess student work. The students need to use these words to talk about their limericks. Candidates need to bear this in mind as they construct their learning segments. The academic language of the standard must be used by the students. I discuss this further in chapter 3 and again in chapter 5.

THINGS TO REMEMBER

- All students will learn. The common core standards or state standards set the required curriculum outcomes but not the prescribed method and content. Lesson plans are designed to reflect a learning segment of a larger unit.

- Learning tasks are well-defined learning outcomes that the candidate writes into the math and literacy lesson plans. Tasks are used as benchmarks throughout the learning segment. Tasks are sequential. The students must master the first task in order to move to the second task. Rubrics are used to measure student progress as they participate in the learning segment.
- Learning objectives need to reflect the common core standards or state standards and should have a specific outcome that students will produce at the end of the learning segment.
- Lesson plans are written plans used to communicate to the evaluator what the candidate will teach in a learning segment.
- Bloom's taxonomy revised (figure 2.3) is the source of all tasks. Each task has a product. Common core standards or state standards set the outcome of the unit and learning segments. The language used in the standard needs to be a stated outcome and thus used by students in both the literacy and math learning segments.

NOTES

1. Beirne, Dianna, and Kathleen Velsor. *Engaging Students: Using the Unit in Comprehensive Lesson Planning.* New York: Rowman & Littlefield Education, 2012. 41–43.

2. Beirne and Velsor, *Engaging Students*, 20–23.

3. Beirne and Velsor, *Engaging Students*, 44.

4. New York State Common Core Standards, www.corestandards.org/ELA-Literacy/WHST.

5. Anderson, Lori, and David Krathwohl. *A Taxonomy of Learning Teaching and Assessing: A Revision of Bloom's Taxonomy of Educational Objectives, Complete Edition.* New York: Longman, 2001. 67–68.

6. Beirne and Velsor, *Engaging Students*, 40.

7. Sheppard Software, www.sheppardsoftware.com/math.htm#geometry.

8. Common Core State Standards Initiative, www.corestandards.org/ELA-Literacy/WHST/6-8/.

3

Lesson Planning

Candidates need to have a lesson plan format that covers the topics listed in figure 3.1. There are thirteen topics that need to be addressed. In chapters 1 and 2, classroom context, learning standards, learning objectives, tasks, instructional strategies, modifications/adaptations, and assessment plans were discussed. In this chapter, procedures are discussed, using tasks as the outline for the lesson.

For the purpose of explaining the format, let's continue with the lesson on poetry for fourth grade students.

SAMPLE LESSON PLAN

Your Name:
Topic: Poetry Unit, Limericks
Level: Grade 4
Estimated Time: 35–45 minutes
Classroom Context: There are twenty-one students in the classroom, thirteen girls and eight boys. Three students have individual education plans (IEPs); one student has attention deficit hyperactivity disorder (ADHD); and four students are English language learners (ELL). All of these students actively participate in lessons through group work, writing buddies, computer-assisted learning. They are able to move around the room if necessary. One student has a full-time aide to assist with the lesson.

Name:

Topic:
Level:
Estimated Time: 35–45 minutes
Classroom Context:
Learning Standards:
Learning Objective:
Learning Tasks:
  • *Remembering*
  • *Understanding*
  • *Applying*
  • *Analyzing*
  • *Evaluating*
Procedures:
  • Hook (a question)
  • I show you/you show me
  • Student work sample
  • Sharing work samples
  • Exit slips
Instructional Strategies:
Modifications/Adaptations:
Assessment Plan:
Materials:
References:

Figure 3.1. Lesson Plan Format

Learning Standards: CCSSELA Literacy RL45—Explain major differences between poems, drama, and prose, and refer to the structural elements of poems (e.g., verse, rhythm, meter) and drama (e.g., cast of characters, settings, descriptions, dialogue, stage directions) when writing or speaking about a text.[1]

Learning Objective: Students will write a limerick and explain the use of meter, rhythm, and rhyme.

Learning Tasks:

  • *Remembering*—Task: List three terms used in poetry.
  • *Remembering*—Task: List three characteristics of a limerick (verse, rhythm, and meter).
  • *Understanding*—Task: Explain the rhythmic pattern of a limerick.
  • *Applying*—Task: Listen to a limerick and explain three characteristics (why it is silly, rhythm, and meter).

- *Analyzing*—Task: Diagram a limerick to demonstrate rhythm and meter.
- *Evaluating*—Task: Write a limerick. Read the limerick to a partner.

Procedures: This will be discussed later in this chapter.

Instructional Strategies: Showing a visual picture of the old man with a beard. This is the limerick used in the example. Re-read the poem and count out the syllables while emphasizing the beat by tapping on the table to demonstrate how meter and rhyme play a role in a limerick.

Modifications/Adaptations: For the four ELL students, using the picture of the old man with the beard will help them to see what the limerick is about. The students may have trouble with the vocabulary words *lark* and *wren*. The picture will show them that they are birds. Also the four students will receive a list of rhyming words with three syllables and examples of limericks. To focus their ideas and to enhance the unique qualities of their South American culture, the candidate will start the limerick with "there once was a man from Ecuador." Walk around to each student and ensure students are writing limericks using the correct measure and rhyme. Allow the three IEP students to work together, use the computer for rhyming words, and take breaks if necessary. Reading teacher will assist with ELL students and less fluent readers.

Students will be assessed informally based on the stated tasks. A rubric has been designed and is in the assessment materials document. Summative assessment will be listening for rhyme, meter, and limerick qualities when the students read their limericks aloud. Students will complete a poetry exit slip.

Materials: Edward Lear's *A Book of Nonsense*, paper, pencil, drum, a picture of the old man with a beard.

PROCEDURES

This segment of the lesson plan is videotaped and submitted to edTPA. The candidate selects one lesson in the learning segment in a sequence of a unit. This learning segment is the second in a unit on poetry. This is discussed further in chapter 5.

The tasks set the sequence of the lesson that the candidate needs to follow. Engaging students in the learning process is extremely important in managing the classroom instruction. The candidate must show enthusiasm for poetry in general and limericks in particular. Every lesson should begin with a question. This helps to engage the students in the learning process and also allows for each student to focus on the task at hand. Piaget referred to this as "disequilibration," the funny, uneasy feeling students experience when they are about to start something exciting and new.[2]

The "Hook"

Carol Tomlinson is credited for coining the term *essential question*.[3] If the candidate decides to use this term in the procedures, it would be to the candidate's benefit to acknowledge this book as a source. In *Engaging Students*, the term *hook* is defined as the question that is designed to set the stage for learning to begin. The concept remains the same.

The candidate begins each lesson with a question that focuses the students on the standard and the purpose of the learning segment. The question is always asked of the students; that is why it is in the procedures section. The candidate should include this segment in the video that is submitted. Submitting the beginning of the learning segment ensures that the evaluator is focused on the objective.

In this learning segment, the candidate is interested in verse, rhythm, and meter as it relates to limericks. What would be a great question? "Girls and boys, have any of you ever heard of a type of poem called a limerick?" Candidate writes *limerick* on the board. The students do not respond. Was that a bad question? No. The candidate now has assessed the students' knowledge of limericks. The candidate can use this in the commentary in the video. This is discussed in chapter 5.

The candidate responds, "I am going to read a limerick and I want you to listen very carefully to the rhythm and the rhyming pattern. Can anyone tell me what is meant by rhythm?" Response: "The beat." "Great! What do we mean when we say a word rhymes?" Response: "Words that rhyme like tree and bee." "What else would rhyme with bee?" "Thee and free!" "Oh gee!" "Good job!"

"This is a poem written by Edward Lear. The title is 'There Was an Old Man with a Beard.' Does everyone have their listening ears on?"

> There was an old man with a beard
> Who said, "It is just as I feared!
> Two owls and a hen,
> Four larks and a wren,
> Have all built nests in my beard."[4]

The first connection needs to be to verse, meter, and rhythm. The candidate makes a connection to the previous lesson and then asks another question.

"Yesterday we talked about meter and verse. Can anyone tell me what we were talking about?"

A student responds: "Yesterday we wrote a haiku, a form of Japanese poetry."

"Yes," the candidate responds, "and what was the meter for the haiku?"

"The first line had five syllables and the second line had seven syllables and the third line had five syllables."

"Wonderful. Did they rhyme?"

"No, just the beats no rhyming."

"Good. Let's look at this limerick again and listen for the syllables in each line."

The candidate then turns on the smartboard (having already gone online to kidzone.com and selected "limericks") and shows the limerick "The Old Man with the Beard" to the class. The site has the poem and a picture of a man with a beard. The candidate reads the poem again, this time tapping on the desk to demonstrate the beats.

"Now let us tap the beat together." As they read the poem again the candidate watches to see if the students are tapping out the beat to the poem.

"What else is different about this type of poem?"

Response: "It is silly because the old man has birds in his beard."

"Good! This is probably not a true story but it would certainly be funny if it was."

The candidate then shows on the smartboard the rules for writing a limerick, for example:

8, 8, 5, 5, 8

The first, second, and fifth lines rhyme with each other and have the same number of syllables (typically eight or nine).

The third and fourth lines rhyme with each other and have the same number of syllables (typically five or six).

"Let's read the poem again. Read only the first line to yourself and tap on your desk. Are there eight or nine syllables? Good, there are eight. What is that called in poetry?"

Response: "The Meter."

"Wonderful."

Take a look at the tasks that were written for this lesson. How many tasks
has the candidate now completed? Checking back, the candidate has completed:

- *Remembering*—Task: List three terms used in poetry.
- *Remembering*—Task: List three characteristics of a limerick (verse,
  rhythm, and meter).
- *Understanding*—Task: Explain the rhythmic pattern of a limerick.
- *Applying*—Task: Listen to a limerick and explain three characteristics
  (why it is silly, rhythm, and meter).

Working with the students directly, the candidate can make an assessment as
to how many students are ready to move on. Magical movements happen in
the classroom. Children learn from each other and enjoy writing limericks.
Modeling the next task helps the students to see what they are being asked
to do. This detail is extremely important when teaching any age group, especially elementary age students.

I Show You/You Show Me[5]

The candidate then suggests that the class writes a limerick together. The
candidate begins, "Generally, limericks start with the same phrase: 'There
once was a . . .' or 'There was a . . .'"

The candidate begins with "There once was a man from Ecuador."

"How many beats?" "Nine. Good. Any suggestions? The next line needs
how many beats? Eight or Nine?" "Good. Does anyone have any ideas for
the next line?"

"Who could do nothing but snore!"

"Great! What is next?"

Response: "Five or six beats."

"Anyone have an idea?"

"Until he ate pie."

The candidate responds, "Oh, where is this going?"

"I tell you no lie."

"That funny old man from Ecuador."

The candidate responds, "That certainly is silly! Does it meet all of the
criteria for a limerick? What is the meter for lines one and two?"

Response: "Eight or nine syllables." The candidate responds, "Good. What is the rhyming pattern?"

"The first, second, and fifth lines rhyme, and the third and fourth lines rhyme." The candidate responds, "Wonderful!"

It is important to transition from modeling to the student work sample gracefully. This can be done by explaining the expectations to the students before handing out materials. Never pass out materials and give directions simultaneously. The minute the candidate is satisfied that the students have completed all of the tasks, then the candidate may quickly transition to the assignment. Otherwise the students will be busy looking at the handout rather than listening, thus wasting time and losing the focus of the lesson.

The candidate needs to practice how to address the students. All too often candidates will say, "hey, guys." Even if the cooperating teacher uses this terminology, it is inappropriate at best. "Boys and girls," "ladies and gentlemen," and even terms such as "friends" can be quick, respectful ways of addressing students. It is important to practice this so that the candidate uses a respectful tone when addressing students when filming for the edTPA.

Making a Smooth Transition to the Work Assignment

"Boys and girls, before we each write our own limericks, it might be helpful to brainstorm some of your ideas by making a list of topics on the board. Can anyone think of any topics?"

"My cat named Jack."

"How would you start your limerick?"

"There once was a cat named Jack."

"Great. What words rhyme with Jack?"

"Words like *lack, back, fact, hack.*"

"Good. Boys and girls, I have a handout for you to complete. Please write your name at the top of the page. Under your name are the general rules for limericks that we just went over. I want you to write your own limerick, starting with either 'there once was a . . .' or 'there was a . . .' You are welcome to use your writing buddies. You will have ten minutes to write your poem. If you have time, you can illustrate the poem. And then we will read them to each other to check for meter and rhyme.

"Does anyone have a question?"

A hand goes up.

"Yes?"

"Do we write the limerick on the paper?"

The candidate responds, "Can anyone answer that question?"

A student responds, "Yes, we are going to write the limerick on the paper, and then if we have time we can illustrate the poem."

If a student asks a question that the candidate believes has been addressed, a strategy for checking for student understanding is to have another student explain the assignment. If this happens and is used in the video clip, the candidate can use this to identify a strategy used in the classroom.

A good rule to follow is that if the candidate has already covered the information asked by a student and the same question is raised again, using a peer of any age to answer the question may be a better way than rephrasing the response. The focus now leaves the candidate and goes to a friend. This is also a great management tool for building respect among students.[6]

While the students are writing, the candidate walks around the room, making sure the students are on task. This is a good time for informal assessment, noting which students can write a limerick and who may be having problems with rhyming and beat. At the end of ten minutes those students who would like to share can read their limericks to the class.

Exit Slips

After all is completed, each student is asked to write an exit slip. This information can be used as a summative assessment for this lesson for the edTPA. The question to ask the students could be "please write what you have learned in the lesson." This summative assessment assists the candidate with data on how many of the students use the words *rhythm* and *meter*; how many remembered the pattern for a limerick; and how many students enjoyed the lesson. This concept is covered in chapter 5.

WHAT DOES THE PROCEDURE LOOK LIKE FOR THE edTPA?

Generally, the candidate is limited by space, and it is important to be clear so that the evaluator can read the procedures quickly and still comprehend how the lesson flows. As of fall 2014, the candidate is limited to four pages for each lesson plan.

A key concept for the edTPA is to make sure that what the candidate actually teaches on the videotape is what is in the lesson plan. The plan and the video lesson need to be the same. Using the tasks as the guide, the candidate stays focused during the learning segment.

The lesson procedures can be simplified by listing the sequence of events. This can be completed in two different ways. One way is to make a list of key points to be covered in the lesson. The second can be a list of actions taken by the candidate and the response made by the students. Both methods provide a clear means of communicating with the evaluator. There is no need to do both.

Using the lesson plan that was just discussed, this is how the procedures could be written in a list form.

Procedures:

1. Essential Question/Hook: Candidate will ask, "Have any of you ever heard of a type of poem called a limerick?" Candidate writes *limerick* on the board.
2. Candidate reviews the meanings of terms meter, rhythm, and rhyme.
3. Candidate reads aloud "There Was an Old Man with a Beard" by Edward Lear.
4. Candidate connects to previous lesson about the meter and rhyme of a haiku.Candidate shows poem with an illustration on the smartboard. The candidate reads the poem again and taps on the desk to demonstrate the meter.
5. The candidate shows the rules of writing a limerick on the smartboard.
6. The candidate asks students to read the first line silently and tap on their desks to find the meter and syllables.
7. The candidate models writing a limerick starting with the phrase, "There once was a man from Ecuador." The students complete the limerick together with the candidate.
8. Students write their own limericks with their writing buddies.
9. Students read their limericks aloud, checking for meter, rhythm, and rhyme.
10. Students complete poetry unit exit slips.

By listing the steps, the evaluator can quickly see the flow of the lesson. It is important that the ten-minute video clip captures some of these elements.

The candidate can choose which ten minutes are important. Data-driven instruction is a key idea for the edTPA. Selecting segments that demonstrate how the candidate is using the ongoing formative assessment during the lesson is important.

THINGS TO REMEMBER

- The lesson plan should include: name, topic, level, estimated time, classroom context, learning standards, learning objective, learning targets (remembering, understanding, applying, analyzing, evaluating), procedures, instructional strategies, modifications/adaptations, assessment plan, and materials.
- The learning objective is related to the common core standard and is the outcome of the lesson.
- Tasks are chosen using Bloom's taxonomy. Tasks are sequential starting with "remembering" for each lesson. The tasks set the sequence for the lesson and act as assessments.
- When selecting the video for the edTPA, candidates must ensure that the tasks in the lesson plan correspond to the action on the video clip.
- Procedures are a list of actions taken by the candidate. Each should be related to the tasks and represent some form of assessment.

NOTES

1. Common Core State Standards Initiative, www.corestandards.org/ELA-Literacy/ WHST/6-8.

2. Wadsworth, Barry J. *Piaget's Theory of Cognitive and Affective Development: Foundations of Constructivism.* 5th ed. White Plains, NY: Longman Publishers, 1971. 19.

3. Tomlinson, Carol Ann, and Jay McTighe. *Integrating Differentiated Instruction Understanding by Design.* Alexandria, VA: Association for Supervision and Curriculum Development, 2006. 20.

4. KidZone Educational Worksheets, www.kidzone.ws/poetry/limerick.htm.

5. Monica Cagney, fourth grade teacher, Locust Valley Intermediate School, Locust Valley, New York.

6. Wadsworth, *Piaget's Theory of Cognitive and Affective Development*, 106.

4

Unit Planning

Common core or state standards set the outcomes for instruction. The candidate is required to design a unit of study based on the standards in literacy and math. Each unit should contain three to five lessons in a learning segment. The cooperating teacher tells the candidate the topic of the units depending on the class schedule and the time allotted to complete each unit.

The candidate needs to be responsive to the needs of the students for the core instruction. The candidate is expected to use the text that the classroom teacher is required to use. Keep in mind that the candidate is a guest in the classroom. The success of the edTPA is based on the candidate's performance in a real situation. This is why the candidate is asked to design a unit using the existing texts and is asked to include formative and summative assessments after each lesson in the learning segment.

ARE THE LITERACY AND MATH UNITS THE SAME?

No. For the literacy unit, the candidate is required to design three lesson plans. The lesson planning format was discussed in chapter 3. The plans are part of a larger unit, and three to five plans represent a learning segment. In most school districts, a text has been adopted by the district. The discussion of the lesson plans is under prompt 3 on the edTPA.

> Describe any district, school, or cooperating teacher requirements or expectations that might affect your planning or delivery of instruction, such as required

curricula, pacing plan, use of specific instructional strategies, or standardized tests.[1]

The candidate needs to tell the evaluator how many hours a day is devoted to literacy. The candidate needs to be honest about the expectations for the candidate in the classroom. The candidate needs to tell the evaluator what text has been adopted. Some texts require the use of the smartboard and video in each lesson. The candidate needs to explain the required instructional strategies. If the school does not have an adopted text, the candidate needs to advise the evaluator that they are responding to the school's adopted response to intervention (RTI) and the common core or state standards. The students in the classroom expect the candidate to use the same instructional plans as the teacher. It is important to keep things the same in this way, so that students know what the expectations are and can respond appropriately.

For example, the candidate may be required to use a scripted text such as *Journeys*.[2] If this is the case, the candidate needs to use the same methodology and simply add to the directions a formative and summative assessment system. A copy of the edTPA test is included in chapter 6. In this example the candidate was bound by certain expectations. The candidate discussed the text selection and added to the already scripted text.

Journeys is one example of an adopted literacy text. Each publisher is bound to the common core standards and therefore has updated its reading programs to incorporate the common core standards. Candidates should be aware that the common core standards or state standards are the basis for the statewide tests. Therefore the texts are designed to assist the students to do well on the exams. The candidate needs to translate the standard into a prescribed unit with three lessons in a learning segment.

Each learning segment follows the prescribed pattern using Bloom's taxonomy. Each task has a student outcome that needs to be satisfied before the learning segment can move forward. The tasks are designed with numbers to enable the student work to be quantified. This allows the candidate to know how many students are prepared to proceed to the next task. For example, the task could ask the students to list five characters from the story.

The task can be measured in a formal or informal way. The students could simply respond verbally—this would be informal—or write a list in their journals, which would be formal. In either case, the candidate can refer to the tasks as indicators of student learning during the commentary of the unit/learning segment assessments for the edTPA.

WHICH LESSON SHOULD BE VIDEOTAPED?

The edTPA requires that the candidate submit a video of the actual classroom teaching experience. This requires permission from the school district. These arrangements need to be made before the candidate is placed in a classroom. Each student is required to have signed permission from a parent or guardian in order to participate in the lesson.

The edTPA evaluators are not looking for a professional film; all that is needed is a tripod and a video camera. The camera should not be in the center of the classroom. Placing the camera on a cabinet or a desk in the back of the room helps the students forget that they are being taped. Some candidates place the camera in the room as early as the first week so that the students become accustomed to the equipment. The students like knowing that they can help the candidate to become a teacher. This can be an enjoyable project for all concerned.

The video is from the literacy unit. Using the lesson plan format discussed in chapter 3 should be helpful to the candidate. The method described assists in the management of the lesson. During the procedures, the candidate can demonstrate to the evaluator how the continuing assessment process works. This was demonstrated in the lesson plan on limericks in chapter 3.

The evaluator is not looking for a complete lesson on the video. The candidate is required to send a ten-minute clip of the learning segment. The candidate needs to highlight the best part of the lesson. The beginning is important: reviewing and checking for remembering and setting up the lesson. The candidate needs to select three sections that tell the evaluator how the lesson was conveyed, thus demonstrating the ongoing assessment process. In the limerick lesson from chapter 3, the candidate could select the section where the candidate made connection to the previous lesson.

The second selection could be modeling using the tapping strategy, and the final clip of the students reading their limericks aloud to the class. It is important that the ten-minute video clip of the learning segment matches the actual lesson plan. The lesson plan may need to be modified after the lesson to reflect what occurs on tape. An elementary classroom is unpredictable, so the candidate needs to be flexible and redirect the learning segment to match the classroom situations. YouTube has many good examples of literacy lessons from elementary classrooms. Watching some of these may help the candidate to see what the expectations are for the video.

HOW CAN THE CANDIDATE DESIGN A LITERACY UNIT?

The first lesson in the unit introduces the students to the unit question. This question should be a large question that connects to the standard and all of the learning segments. In the example in chapter 3, the candidate was introduced to a lesson on poetry. The learning segment was about limericks. The unit question could be "What is poetry?" or "What are different types of poetry?" Both are good questions. The question selected would be the source for each of the learning segments.[3]

The candidate is expected to videotape one of the lessons in the learning segment in the literacy unit. The first lesson can be used to collect data for the second lesson in the learning segment. Using the second lesson for the video assessment places the candidate in a good position to use the assessment from the first to plan the next lesson. In candidate's exam in chapter 6, the first lesson in the learning segment is a vocabulary lesson. The second lesson is a comprehension lesson using historical fiction as a platform for explaining the concept of finding evidence in the text.

The candidate began the lesson by reviewing the previous lesson in the segment. The candidate reviewed the vocabulary by defining historical fiction and then reviewed text evidence to check for understanding from the students. The candidate used the second lesson for the video. The second lesson began with a review and set the learning experience for the comprehension lesson using evidence to support an explanation of the reading selection. The students completed a comprehension worksheet. The worksheet was used as an example of student work samples.

IS THIS THE SAME PROCESS FOR THE MATH UNIT?

In the math unit, the candidate is required to list the central focus of the unit, identifying the common core or state standards. The candidate is asked to complete a chart for each learning segment. Under each labeled section, the candidate is asked to list learning objectives for each lesson. Next to this list, the candidate is asked to list the instructional strategies and learning tasks. In another column, the candidate is asked to cite formative and summative assessments. This is discussed further in chapter 5.

Go Math!⁴ is an example of one type of math curriculum used by some districts. Each lesson identifies the common core standard and includes a video and worksheets for the student. The candidate needs to translate the classroom text or the standards into a unit with three to five lessons using Bloom's taxonomy for continual assessment of student learning.

HOW CAN THE CANDIDATE BEGIN THE MATH UNIT?

In chapter 2, the candidate was introduced to a learning segment on parallelograms. This was the fourth lesson in the learning segment in the unit. The first lesson introduces the question "What are quadrilaterals?" The first lesson in the learning segment defines the next three lessons. Each lesson builds on completed tasks from the previous learning segment. Each lesson includes tasks that students must achieve. Setting tasks to each level of Bloom's taxonomy assists the candidate in assessing student learning.

Tasks are given a qualifying number, such as "students will list six polygons." If eighteen out of twenty students can list the names of the polygons, the candidate can then ask the students to label or draw an example of each shape. If ten students cannot remember the difference between a hexagon and a pentagon, the candidate can report that 50 percent of the students need instruction on pentagons and hexagons. When discussing this on the edTPA, the candidate could say, "The research shows that 50 percent of the students needed a mini-lesson or simply a new strategy to identify the difference between a hexagon and a pentagon." The students would not need a reengagement lesson, just a new strategy.

WHAT IS A REENGAGEMENT LESSON?

If a large percentage of students could not master the tasks taught in the core instruction as evidenced by the incorrect answers on their worksheets, then a reengagement lesson would be necessary. Using the Bloom's taxonomy for assessment purposes helps the candidate to make a decision as to what needs to be retaught in a different way. A reengagement lesson needs to use a different set of strategies than those used in the core instruction. Shouting at students because they did not understand the lesson the first time does not change the instruction.

Figure 4.1.   Shouting at Students Does Not Change the Instruction.

HOW DOES DATA DRIVE THE NEXT LEARNING SEGMENT?

In the edTPA the candidate needs to identify tasks that produce student work samples. The student work samples are the benchmarks for accomplishing each task. The final work sample is the outcome of instruction and should achieve the stated goal of the common core standard. For the edTPA, the candidate must present and critique a final work sample from three different students from one of the math lessons. This is discussed in chapter 5.

The outcome for all students in this standard grade 3 section A1 in geometry is to

CCSS.MATH.CONTENT.3.G.A.1: Understand that shapes in different categories (e.g., rhombuses, rectangles, and others) may share attributes (e.g., having four sides) and that the shared attributes can define a larger category (e.g., quadrilaterals). Recognize rhombuses, rectangles, and squares as examples of quadrilaterals, and draw examples of quadrilaterals that do not belong to any of these subcategories.

The standard begins with the word "understand." Reviewing figure 2.3, this means that students construct meaning from oral, graphic, or written messages. Students can explain, summarize, generalize, interpret, infer, paraphrase, and classify. This can be accomplished through a report, illustration, matching chart, demonstration, and dramatization. The outcome of our unit will be to illustrate six quadrilaterals and label each one according to the types of intersecting lines.

If the first lesson in the learning segment in the math unit is about quadrilaterals, the unit questions could be "What are quadrilaterals?" and "How are they the same and how are they different?" The first lesson should address key words (academic language) that the students need to remember before they study the quadrilateral family: students will need to remember concepts from a previous unit on intersecting lines. Without this knowledge, they will not be able to explain the similarities and differences among the quadrilaterals.[5]

After the students have demonstrated that they remember these terms, they then can explain different quadrilaterals using those terms. The standard asks that the students recognize and draw examples of rectangles, squares, rhombuses, parallelograms, trapezoids, and kites.

> Each drawing should be labeled with the terms.
>
> The Learning Segment: What are quadrilaterals? How are they the same and how are they different?
>
> Lesson 1: Reviewing different types of lines
> Lesson 2: What makes a quadrilateral?
> Lesson 3: Reengagement lesson on quadrilaterals
> Lesson 4: What is a parallelogram?

Under the section titled "math overview" on the edTPA, the candidate is asked to

> Briefly describe the instruction preceding the assessment by typing within the brackets in each section of the chart below (no more than two single-spaced pages). Do not delete or alter the chart; both the chart and your description are included in the total page count allowed. Refer to the evidence chart in the

handbook to ensure that this document complies with all format specifications. Pages exceeding the maximum will not be scored.[6]

In each learning segment, the edTPA requires a statement of the central focus: "The focus of this learning segment will be to illustrate six quadrilaterals and to label each one according to the types of intersecting lines." Next, the edTPA asks the candidate to list the common core or state standards.

Underneath the central focus is the first lesson. The key statement in the directions is: "Briefly describe the instruction preceding assessment by typing within the brackets below (no more than two single-spaced pages)." How can the candidate do this?

The candidate should write a lesson plan using the model from chapter 3. After the lesson plan is finished, the candidate can select the lists of tasks and the procedures and complete the form. In the procedure section, the candidate needs to identify the strategies used to accomplish the learning segment.

A strategy is the candidate's approach to the lesson. For example, the strategies for the lesson on lines noted in table 4.1 is: the candidate prepared cards for each term and posted them on the board during instruction and designed a poster with examples. Candidate will review each term. The strategy to facilitate student learning was: Students will draw lines and label drawing. Students will write definitions in journals. Students will list five examples of perpendicular lines.

This is the plan for instruction and it also lists the outcomes. Underneath this is a brief retelling of the procedures using student voices. The candidate can simply list the procedures depending on space.

Candidate will ask each student to draw with their ruler three lines straight across their paper.

Candidate: These lines are parallel. What do you think this means?

Student: They never touch?

Candidate: Parallel lines are lying on the same plane and never touch. Good job. *Posts the card with "parallel" on the board.*

Turn your paper sideways. Use your ruler to make three parallel lines across your paper. The candidate demonstrates.

Candidate: These lines are intersecting. What does this mean?

Student: They cut across like a checkerboard.

Candidate: Label the lines that are intersecting. Are they parallel lines, too?

Student: Yes. *The candidate posts the card with "intersecting" on the board.*

Candidate: When angles intersect it is called perpendicular. Can someone explain to the class what this means?

Student: When they cross and make a right angle.

Candidate: Can anyone find any lines that are perpendicular in the classroom?

Please write in your journal what parallel lines are. What intersecting lines are. List five examples of perpendicular lines in the classroom. This is the instruction prior to assessment.

This is the formative and summative assessment plan:

Formative assessment—Students will draw six lines and label the drawing with three words: parallel, intersection, perpendicular. Students will write three definitions in their journals. Students will list five examples of perpendicular lines.

If a student can't label and define the terms, then the candidate can redirect the student's thinking using a new strategy or mini-lesson.

WHAT IS THE SUMMATIVE ASSESSMENT?

Students complete an exit slip about what they learned today.

WHAT DOES THE REENGAGEMENT LESSON LOOK LIKE?

The edTPA requires that the candidate design a reengagement lesson. This example uses lesson 3 as the reengagement lesson. The key idea here is that the core instruction was successful for some students but not all students. This happens in the best classrooms.

The candidate needs to identify how they know their students need another lesson. The candidate needs to address this using the format provided in chapter 2 so that the evaluator is aware of the criteria used. In the example in table 4.1, the assessment statement under "strategy" is: "(Reengagement

Table 4.1. Math Overview. The edTPA requires that the candidate organize the unit in the following manner:

The Central Focus Similarities and differences of quadrilaterals.	Common core or state standard CCSS.MATH.CONTENT.3.G.A.1 Understand that shapes in different categories (e.g., rhombuses, rectangles, and others) may share attributes (e.g., having four sides), and that the shared attributes can define a larger category (e.g., quadrilaterals). Recognize rhombuses, rectangles, and squares as examples of quadrilaterals, and draw examples of quadrilaterals that do not belong to any of these subcategories.	
Learning Segment	Learning Objective	Instructional strategies Learning tasks	Formative and summative assessments
L1	Students will identify and draw parallel, intersecting, and perpendicular lines.	Strategies: Candidate (C) prepared cards for each term and designed a poster with examples. C will review each term. Students (S) will draw lines and label drawing. S will write definitions in journals. S will list five examples of perpendicular lines. C will ask each student to draw with their ruler three lines straight across their paper. C: These lines are parallel what do you think this means? S: They never touch? C: Parallel lines are lying on the same plane and never touch. Good job. *Posts the card with "parallel" on the board.* Turn your paper sideways. Using your ruler make 3 parallel lines across your paper. C demonstrates. These lines are intersecting. What does this mean? S: They cut across like a checkerboard. C: Label the lines that are intersecting. Are they parallel lines, too? S: Yes. *Post the card with "intersecting" on the board.* C: When angles intersect it is called perpendicular. Can someone explain to the class what this means? S: When they cross and make a right angle. C: Can anyone find any lines that are perpendicular in the classroom? Please write in your journal what parallel lines are. What intersecting lines are. List five examples of perpendicular lines in the classroom.	*Formative assessment* Students will draw six lines and label drawing with three words: parallel, intersection, perpendicular. Students will write three definitions in journals. Students will list five examples of perpendicular lines. If the students cannot label and define the terms, then the candidate can redirect student thinking using a new strategy or mini-lesson. *Summative assessment* Students will complete an exit slip about what they learned today.

L2	Students will construct quadrilaterals and draw examples of each: rectangles, squares, rhombuses, parallelograms, trapezoids, and kites. Each drawing should be labeled with the terms.	Strategies: C will make a square using four straws and glue this to a piece of cardboard. C will label the drawing to define the lines: parallel, intersecting, and perpendicular. S will construct six quadrilaterals using straws of different lengths. S will sort the quadrilaterals according to properties. S will draw and label each shape on the graph provided. C will identify six types of quadrilaterals and ask: which have parallel, intersecting, and perpendicular lines? C will tell students that they will be making quadrilaterals—four-sided shapes—with straws of different lengths. They will make the first with four of the same color and length; the second with three of the same color and one different length; the third with two of the same color and another two of the same color; the fourth with two of the same colors and two of different colors; and fifth all of different colors. They will need to make the shapes and record them on the graph provided.	*Formative assessment* *Remembering:* Students verbally remember definitions of lines and apply to the quadrilaterals. *Understanding:* Students will make six shapes according to the directions. *Applying:* Students will correctly label their drawings. *Summative assessment* The completed worksheet and exit slips.
L3	Students will be able to identify quadrilaterals that are the same and different.	Strategy: (Reengagement lesson) 50 percent of the students did not explain parallelogram, trapezoid, rhombus, and kite. C needs to reintroduce and define quadrilaterals. Have students come individually to draw and label each one on the smartboard. Ask students to watch a YouTube video[1] to see if they can identify the shapes and their names. Students will complete matching worksheets—Students will share their responses with a buddy.	*Formative assessment* Students will draw and label each quadrilateral. Students answer questions from the video. *Summative assessment* Students will complete a "same and different" worksheet and exit slips.

[1] Identify Quadrilaterals (Geometry): Third Grade Splash Math, YouTube, www.youtube.com/watch?v=IQE6yEsRNAM.

lesson) 50 percent of the students did not explain parallelogram, trapezoid, rhombus, and kite."

It is important to change the strategy if the original method using straws to make their own models did not work. The candidate can begin by reintroducing and defining quadrilaterals to 50 percent of the instructional core. The new strategy would be to have students individually draw and label each quadrilateral on the smartboard. Ask students to watch a YouTube video to see if they can identify the shapes and their names. Students complete matching worksheets[7] and share their responses with their neighbors. When all of the students have completed the identification of quadrilaterals, then the candidate can introduce the last lesson on parallelograms. As of fall 2014, candidates must send three graded work samples and the scoring rubric from the reengagement lesson.

THINGS TO REMEMBER

- The common core or state standards set the outcomes for instruction.
- Candidates need to be responsive to the needs of all students for the core instruction.
- The literacy unit requires three to five lesson plans.
- Candidates need to add the assessment model from chapter 2 to the required text.
- Candidates need to explain the literacy program to the evaluator, including the number of hours devoted to literacy each day.
- Candidates need to select one lesson to videotape.
- Candidates need to select three different segments for a total of ten minutes.
- Tasks need to be designed with numbers to quantify student learning outcomes.
- The math unit is placed into a form on the edTPA.
- The candidate needs to identify learning objectives, instructional strategies, and learning tasks.
- Learning tasks need to be listed with numbers in order to quantify student learning outcomes.
- Candidates are limited to two single-spaced pages on the edTPA. Follow the directions!

- Instructional strategies refers to the candidate's instructional plan. Candidates need to select work samples from three students to critique after both the core instruction and the reengagement lesson.
- Learning tasks are student outcomes; they need to be identified as formative or summative assessments.

NOTES

1. Education Teaching Performance Assessment (edTPA), prompt 3.

2. *Journeys*. Boston, MA: Houghton Mifflin Harcourt Publishing, 2014.

3. Beirne, Dianna, and Kathleen Velsor. *Engaging Students: Using the Unit in Comprehensive Lesson Planning*. New York: Rowman & Littlefield Education, 2012. 52–58.

4. Houghton Mifflin Harcourt, *Go Math! Standards Practice Book, Common Core Edition*, 2011.

5. www.math-lesson-plans.com/geometry.html.

6. Education Teaching Performance Assessment (edTPA), "Math Overview."

7. Identify Quadrilaterals (Geometry): 3rd Grade Splash Math, YouTube.

5

Assessment

Assessment-driven instruction is the model used to respond to the No Child Left Behind (NCLB) Act of 2001: every classroom instructional plan should be designed to ensure that all students make adequate yearly progress in literacy and math.[1] The response to intervention (RTI) was discussed in chapter 1. The RTI is a means for school districts to comply with this legislation.

The RTI provides the framework for literacy development for each student in every school. Classroom teachers must be in compliance with the stated benchmarks for literacy and math. These changes have already occurred in the classrooms where candidates will be placed. The cooperating teacher is accountable for each student's progress in literacy and math.

ASSESSMENTS' MOST IMPORTANT PURPOSE IS NOT TO PROVE INSTRUCTION BUT TO IMPROVE INSTRUCTION[2]

The edTPA is a performance-based assessment of teacher candidates' abilities to design and execute learning segments using student assessment data. The exam is designed to evaluate the candidates' familiarity with the RTI in their schools. The RTI is a tool for instruction. The RTI can provide the candidate information about the school and about the students' progress in the classroom.

Each learning segment is tied to a standard, which is connected to a series of tasks for students to achieve in order to meet the standard. Thus, each learning segment is assessed according to certain prescribed criteria. Students are assessed based on the outcomes of the lesson. Learning segments are then modified to address the needs of the students in each classroom.

Designing learning segments that are parts of continuous units of study allows the candidate to assess student progress over the course of three to five lessons. Student progress is linked to the continual assessments of each task during every lesson in every learning segment in every unit. This is the key idea behind the edTPA.

WHAT ASSESSMENT IS THE CANDIDATE REQUIRED TO ADDRESS?

In task 3, "assessing students' literacy learning," there are four corresponding assessments that each candidate needs to address. The first is the academic assessment of the students that the candidate uses to perform the lessons in the learning segment. The second is the formative assessment of one lesson in the literacy segment that the candidate videotapes. The third is the formative assessment of student work samples. The fourth is the summative assessment of the lesson as demonstrated in the exit slips and class work or homework assignments.[3] Examples of these assessments are provided in chapter 6.

In task 4, "assessing students' mathematics learning," there are four corresponding assessments that the candidate needs to address. The first is an assessment of the whole class for core instruction. The second formative assessment is to identify one area where students struggle mathematically. This should be demonstrated through three student work samples. The students should represent tier II and III learners. Third is the formative assessment of three student work samples. The summative assessment of the lesson is demonstrated in the exit slip and homework assignment. The fourth is the design of the reengagement lesson for tier II and tier III students, which is assessed through student work samples and exit slips. Examples of the four assessments are in chapter 6.

In fall 2014, two additional assessments were added. The candidate is asked to assess a lesson in the learning segment that then becomes the basis for the reengagement lesson. The candidate is asked to assess student work samples at the end of the core instruction and at the end of the reengagement lesson.[4]

WHAT IS THE DIFFERENCE BETWEEN
FORMATIVE AND SUMMATIVE ASSESSMENT?

In chapter 3 the candidate learned how to design lessons that facilitate the continual assessment process. Each lesson has an objective that is aligned with the common core standards. Task assessments are designed to follow Bloom's taxonomy. Each lesson begins with remembering.

The candidate needs to know what the students remember about the previous learning segment and topic before beginning instruction. This type of assessment is call formative assessment. The assessment informs the candidate about what the students know before instruction begins and continues throughout the instruction. Knowing what students remember guides the lesson to the next level of understanding. Designing tasks that are quantitative and aligned to the objective and the standards provides the candidate with information that can be used as data about student learning during class instruction.

Summative assessments are used at the end of the lesson. Summative means "summing up" the data. The Bloom's taxonomy rubric provides summative information. Student homework samples, exit slips, and homework assignments can provide summative information.

The summative data is used to design the next lesson. Student work samples also provide formative assessments. These can be either informal or formal work samples that provide information during the learning segment.

HOW CAN THE CANDIDATE IMPROVE THE USE
OF ACADEMIC LANGUAGE IN THE ASSESSMENTS?

There are some useful academic terms that may assist the candidate to embellish the commentary of the lesson plan prompt 3, the math overview, and the video clip. Terms such as *diagnostic*, *alternative*, *authentic*, and *performance assessment* can be used in formative or summative assessments.[5]

Diagnostic assessment is a term used to identify what the students already know or may need to learn in order to succeed in the core instruction of the classroom setting. The candidate might design a math worksheet where each problem identifies a particular skill; for example, in the first lesson of the math unit on quadrilaterals, the students need to know the definition of parallel and intersecting lines.

If on their exit slips 100 percent of the students know what parallel lines are but only 50 percent demonstrate an understanding of intersecting lines, the candidate could write: "This was a diagnostic summative assessment."

The summative assessment diagnosed that 50 percent of the students did not know and could not explain what intersecting lines are. The candidate could then design a mini-lesson using a different strategy or a learning center for those students to demonstrate their knowledge of intersecting lines.

Alternative assessment and authentic assessment are terms used to describe an assessment where students are asked to demonstrate what they have learned in a real-life situation. For example, the candidate might design a lesson for first graders about currency and use actual money to purchase items in the classroom and to make change. The candidate could refer to the assessment as an authentic assessment of the student's ability to make change for a $1 bill or $5 bill.

Performance assessment is a term applied to student work samples. It is a form of assessment where the student is asked to perform rather than to answer questions on a test. Unlike diagnostic assessments, performance assessments are designed to have students demonstrate their work. Having the students read their limericks aloud to hear the rhythm and rhyme is an example of a performance assessment.

In the limerick lesson, the term *performance assessment* may enhance the candidate's response to the question on the edTPA.[6] This can occur during the learning segment (formative assessment) or after homework assignment, which would be a summative performance assessment.[7]

In a broad sense, the edTPA is considered to be a performance assessment in that the candidate must demonstrate instructional competencies through the use of the video, written lesson plans, unit design, math overview, and student work samples.

HOW CAN THE CANDIDATE DEMONSTRATE THE ASSESSMENT OF STUDENT LEARNERS IN THE CLASSROOM?

In the lesson plan format for the learning segment, the candidate is asked to discuss modifications and adaptations for the students in the classroom. In chapter 6, the candidate listed these modifications based on the assessment of the students in the learning segment. The candidate provides audio text, targeted guided reading, guided questioning, cooperative learning groups with peers, and new vocabulary in context and allows room for oral assessment and uses actions and gestures to explain unfamiliar words.

HOW CAN THE CANDIDATE ASSESS STUDENT LEARNING DURING THE LEARNING SEGMENT?

A formative assessment can be completed as students participate in the core instruction of the learning segment. The candidate needs to assess student learning. This is accomplished through the use of a rubric. The candidate can use either formal or informal means to assess student learning. An informal formative assessment can be a checklist for each student and each task. A formal formative assessment can be having the students write a sentence to explain a vocabulary word.

In the lesson on limericks, there are a number of assessments. Some are formal and some are informal.

1. Essential Question/Hook: Candidate asks, "Have any of you ever heard of a type of poem called limericks?" (Informal assessment.) Candidate writes *limerick* on the board.
2. Candidate reviews the meanings of the terms meter, rhythm, and rhyme. (Informal assessment.)
3. Candidate reads aloud the limerick "There Was an Old Man with a Beard" by Edward Lear. (Informal assessment.)
4. Candidate connects limerick lesson to a prior lesson about haikus. (Informal assessment.)
5. Candidate shows poem with an illustration on the smartboard. The candidate reads the poem again and taps on the desk to demonstrate the meter. (Informal assessment.)
6. Candidate shows the rules for writing a limerick on the smartboard. (Informal assessment.)
7. Candidate asks students to read the first line silently and to tap on their desk to find meter and syllables. (Informal assessment.)

8. Candidate models writing a limerick starting with the phrase, "There once was a man from Ecuador." The students complete the limerick together with the candidate. (Informal assessment.)
9. Students write their own limerick with their writing buddies. (Informal assessment.)
10. Students read their limericks aloud, checking for meter, rhythm, and rhyme (Summative assessment.)
11. Students complete poetry unit exit slips. (Summative assessment.)

If during the core instruction a student or a group of students does not achieve the task, the candidate can redirect the lesson using a short mini-lesson with a different strategy to bring those students to the level of the core instruction. This can be done by rephrasing a question, drawing a diagram, restating a concept in a different way, or simply restating and asking another student to explain the concept.

When the candidate uses this approach in the video, it should be identified as an assessment and explained to the evaluator as to why the candidate redirected the learning segment based on the instructional rubric.

HOW TO USE THE INSTRUCTIONAL
RUBRIC IN THE VIDEO COMMENTARY

The candidate is allowed six single-spaced pages to respond to a series of questions. In reviewing the responses, it is useful to refer to the scoring rubric in the edTPA handbook.[8] The questions are tricky and use academic language that may be confusing to the candidate. The following responses are derived from the literacy segment on limericks. There are four categories: promoting a positive learning environment, engaging students in learning, deepening student learning during instruction, and analyzing teaching.

How does the candidate demonstrate a positive learning environment that exhibits rapport and respect for students? The candidate began the lesson by asking the students, "Girls and boys, have you ever heard of a limerick?" The candidate then wrote *limerick* on the board. The students did not respond. This is an opportunity to highlight how the candidate used the essential question or hook to access prior knowledge.

Standard ELA RL 45	Unacceptable Tier III (reengagement lesson for five students)	Acceptable Tier II (new strategy)	Target Core Instruction Tier I	
Remembering	Five students can list three terms used in poetry.	Students can list three terms used in poetry.	Students can list three terms used in poetry.	
Remembering	Five students can list three characteristics of poetry: verse, rhythm, and meter.	Fifteen students can list three characteristics of poetry: verse, rhythm, and meter.	Twenty students can list three characteristics of poetry: verse, rhythm, and meter.	
Understanding	After listening to a limerick, five students can tap out the meter and verbally explain three characteristics: rhythm, meter, and "silly."	After listening to a limerick, fifteen students can tap out the meter and verbally explain three characteristics: rhythm, meter, and "silly."	After listening to a limerick, twenty students can tap out the meter and verbally explain three characteristics: rhythm, meter, and "silly."	
Applying	After listening to a limerick, five students can tap out the meter and verbally explain three characteristics: rhythm, meter, and "silly."	After listening to a limerick, fifteen students can tap out the meter and verbally explain three characteristics: rhythm, meter, and "silly."	After listening to a limerick, twenty students can tap out the meter and verbally explain three characteristics: rhythm, meter, and "silly."	
Applying	Five students complete the limerick together.	Fifteen students complete the limerick together.	Twenty students complete the limerick together.	
Analyzing	Five students write their own limericks with writing buddies.	Fifteen students write their own limericks with writing buddies.	Twenty students write their own limericks with writing buddies.	
Evaluating	Five students read limericks aloud and complete exit slips.	Fifteen students read limericks aloud and complete exit slips.	Twenty students read limericks aloud and complete exit slips.	

Figure 5.1.   Instructional Limerick Rubric

The candidate continued in a positive way and said, "I am going to read a limerick and I want you to listen to the rhythm and rhyming pattern." This identifies the purpose for the reading of the poem. This is a literacy strategy. The candidate continued by saying, "Can anyone tell me what is meant by *rhythm*? A student raises his hand and says, "Beat."

The candidate responded, "Great." This is a respectful, positive response. Saying something like "Oh, come on, we just learned this yesterday!" is a negative response and does not help to build a positive learning environment. The candidate then asked "what do we mean when we say a word rhymes?" Response: "words that rhyme like tree and bee." "Good."

The candidate can refer to the instructional rubric to support the learning sequence. The candidate's expectation was that the students should know the definition of rhythm and rhyme before proceeding. This is respectful to all students and should be highlighted here.

The candidate is also asked to explain how this lesson is respectful to children of other cultures. In the class description, the candidate identified that there were two aides who helped with students with individual education plans (IEPs) and six English language learners (ELL) students.

The response should include a discussion of how the candidate used the smartboard to illustrate the silly limerick for students with attention difficulties and for students whose second language is English. The picture helped the students to see the words in the poem. This can be a good argument for challenging students to engage in learning. The visual picture helped the students to see the silly poem. The candidate's response could include any statements offered by the students at that time that supports a positive learning environment.

The candidate is asked to explain to the evaluator how the instruction engaged students in developing an essential literacy strategy and requisite skills. First, the question is asking the candidate to explain how the lesson helped to achieve the standard. In this example the candidate selected common core English language arts (ELA) standard RL45. The students are required to learn poetry with an emphasis on verse, rhythm, and meter.

The essential literacy strategy in this lesson is learning how to independently write a limerick. The evaluator is asking the candidate to explain how the lesson provided the students with a learning experience about rhythm and rhyme so that they can construct their own strategy for writing a limerick. The second part of the question is requisite skills. Requisite skills are the skills that the students "developed and practiced" during the learning segment.[9]

The candidate needs to focus on verse, rhythm, and rhyme. The candidate used KidZone and selected limericks to illustrate "The Old Man with the Beard." The candidate read the poem again and tapped out the beats on the desk. This is rhythm. The candidate then asked the class to tap the beat together as they all read the poem. Reference can be made again to the informal instructional assessment rubric.

The candidate then showed on the smartboard the rules for writing a limerick, for example, the mnemonic device 8, 8, 5, 5, 8. The first, second, and fifth lines rhyme with each other and have the same number of syllables (typically eight or nine; this is meter). The third and fourth lines rhyme with each other and have the same number of syllables (typically five or six; this is meter).

The candidate then asked the students to read the limerick by themselves and tap out the beat. These are requisite skills. Again, a reference can be made to the instructional rubric and the need for an informal assessment at this time to check for student understanding. Tapping helps the students to develop a strategy for writing their own limerick, and this should be acknowledged here. If the classroom aide helped the IEP or ELL students, the candidate should mention this in the commentary.

The second part of this question asks the candidate to describe how the instruction linked to the student's prior knowledge, culture, and community and assisted with learning. The candidate made a connection to the previous lesson in the unit on poetry. "Yesterday we talked about meter and verse. Can anyone tell me what we were talking about?" A student responded, "Yesterday we wrote a haiku, a form of Japanese poetry."

The candidate responded, "What was the meter for a haiku?" The student responded, "The first line had five syllables and the second line had seven syllables and the third line had five syllables." "Wonderful!" the candidate responded, "Did they rhyme?" "No, just beats. No rhyming."

This is indeed a fortunate response. The student has explained to the candidate a clear understanding of the requisite skills needed to write a haiku. To better ensure this response, a simple chart can be placed on the board from the earlier lesson, and if the students can't remember all of the criteria, they can be guided through the chart.

The second part of the question is focused on connecting the lesson to the cultures in the classroom. The candidate modeled how to write a limerick by starting with a man from Ecuador. This example can also be used to support deepening student learning. Modeling is essential to help engage students in the task.

Candidates are asked to explain how they modeled the essential literacy strategy and supported students as they practiced and applied the strategy in a meaningful context. This example of working as a class to write a silly limerick about the man from Ecuador can apply to both and should be explained in both contexts.

Candidates are asked to discuss how they worked to elicit student responses to promote thinking and to apply the essential strategy and requisite skills to compose text. The candidate should discuss the instructional literacy rubric, highlighting the students' reading of the limericks to their writing buddies and to the class.

As the students read their work, the candidate should respond to the meter, rhythm, and rhyme of the students' limericks as they read them. This helps to create a positive learning environment and to support the concept for the essential literacy strategy. The more the students are animated, the more the learning environment is enhanced.

At the end of the lesson the candidate needs to provide the students with exit slips. This provides a summative assessment of the lesson and helps to evaluate whether the students have the essential literacy strategies to write another limerick. The candidate can request that students "write three characteristics of a limerick" and include their names on the exit slips. If each student in the class responds, this could provide good information for the candidate to discuss in this section.

The last component asks for the candidate to analyze their teaching, reflecting on those students who struggled with the assignment and explaining how the candidate may have improved the instruction or may have missed an opportunity with a student. The candidate can refer to the exit slips if appropriate. The students' names are on the slips and they could provide information to the candidate about what was learned.

The candidate should also review the videotape and discuss in a positive way any deviation that may have occurred. The candidate can refer to the instructional literacy rubric as a criterion for the discussion. A possible example may be if the candidate noticed on the video that a student did not have the beat during the independent reading.

During the instruction the candidate did not see this; however, this explains why the student had difficulty writing the limerick. The student did not have all of the requisite skills necessary to write a limerick. In the future, the candidate could pair the student with another student or watch him more carefully to make sure he can imitate the rhythm.

The candidate may also want to mention the work of Howard Gardner and multiple intelligence,[10] which suggests that if students who employ different types of intelligences work together, they are more likely to remember the essential literacy strategy.

The next prompt asks the candidate to attach student work samples with a commentary. In the literacy learning segment on limericks, the student work samples could be their poems. The assessment needs to highlight the essential literacy strategy and the requisite skills. The poem and a discussion of the student samples could demonstrate essential literacy strategy and requisite skills needed to write a limerick. The exit slips can also provide data: if 90 percent of the students knew three characteristics of a limerick, this may be a good indicator of a successful lesson.

The candidate must select three work samples from the class. These samples represent the students in core instruction (tier I), tier II, and tier III instruction. These are referred to as "patterns of learning" in the classroom. The candidate needs to use an assessment rubric to grade the assignment and then to write the assessment criteria for improvement on the work sample.

This can also be completed on videotape or audiotape, depending on the work sample. The candidate needs to attach the scoring rubric and discuss a course of action for each student. The candidate needs to keep the commentary discussion directed toward achieving the standard. In this example it was RL45 poetry: meter, rhythm, and rhyme. Stay on the path!

The candidate needs to discuss qualitative and quantitative data about the student work samples across the three examples. The exit slip asked for three characteristics of a limerick. Numbers provide quantitative results. The rubric used to assess meter, rhythm, and rhyme can provide the candidate with qualitative data. The candidate can analyze the vocabulary, the images, and the silliness of the criteria that were discussed during the lesson and that are part of the rubric that was designed using Bloom's taxonomy.

Standard	Unacceptable 1	Acceptable 2	Target 3	Score
CCSSELA RL45	(Reengagement Lesson)	(New strategy)		
Meter	Does not use syllables but uses words.	Uses syllables and missing rhyming or uses rhyming and needs help with syllables.	First, second, and fifth lines have the same number of syllables (eight or nine); third and fourth lines have the same number of syllables (five or six).	
Rhyme	No rhyming.	Two lines rhyme.	First, second, and fifth lines rhyme; third and fourth lines rhyme.	
Rhythm	Does not read the limerick with the necessary meter.	Reads meter with rhyme or beat.	Reads using the meter and rhyme.	
Silly	No image, just words.	Is not silly.	Poem is not real; it shows imagination and is funny.	

Figure 5.2.   Limerick Assessment Rubric
Source: Jessica Spero

The candidate needs to reflect on this data to design a reengagement lesson for students who could not write a limerick. This information needs to be incorporated into future lessons about poetry. The candidate needs to use the academic language of meter, rhythm, and rhyme in the feedback to students and in the future lesson plans. The academic language is embedded in the standard. Finally, the candidate is asked to make a connection to the next lesson in the learning segment to improve the essential learning strategy and the requisite skills.

Theoretically, if the students mastered the use of rhyme but demonstrated a need to develop content, perhaps the next lesson would be to write a ballad about the school. Ballads always have the same refrain and each verse is part of a continuing story. The class could create the refrain together and individually or in pairs write a verse.

HOW TO COMPLETE THE MATH ASSESSMENT COMMENTARY

In the math assessment commentary, the candidate is asked to identify "specific learning objectives and standards measured by the assessment you chose for analysis." In the learning segment on geometric shapes, the candidate chose the math common core standard 3G1:

> Reason with shapes and their attributes. Understand that shapes in different categories (e.g., rhombuses, rectangles, and others) may share the attributes (e.g., having four sides) and the shared attributes can define a larger category (e.g., quadrilaterals). Recognize rhombuses, rectangles, and squares as examples of parallelograms and draw examples of quadrilaterals that do not belong to any of these categories.

In lesson 4, the candidate chose the learning objective from the MCCS 3G1: Students will draw four parallelograms and label three characteristics. Therefore the assessments are derived from the list of tasks the student completed to be able to draw and label four shapes. The candidate is then asked to provide a graph (chart or table) or a narrative that summarizes student learning for the whole class.

The candidate is then asked to divide the summary into patterns of learning. The patterns referred to are (1) conceptual understanding; (2) procedural fluency; (3) mathematical reasoning/problem-solving skills.[11]

Conceptual understanding is in the math common core standard (MCCS) 3G1: Students will draw four parallelograms and label three characteristics. In the first pattern, the key word is *understanding*. In the second task (understanding) in lesson 4, the students were asked to "summarize their own words three characteristics of a parallelogram." This can be demonstrated in a chart or in a narrative. This data is needed for the next section on procedural fluency.

Procedural fluency refers to the qualitative use of the instructional design. During the instruction, the candidate saw that some of the students had difficulty defining the terms. One suggestion was to have tier I students work with other students to explain the concepts.

Another suggestion was to redirect the students to a visual poster on the wall that lists the characteristics of shapes and to ask those students to find four examples that may apply. Fluency is more than memorizing facts and procedures.[12] Fluency builds on conceptual understanding and strategic reasoning and problem solving, and thus refers to the exploration and discussion of the learning process for all of the students in the core instruction. The candidate can refer to the instructional rubric to compile data regarding the number of students who succeeded on the first attempt and to discuss how these students assisted other students with the lesson. There needs to be a reference to the student aides in the classroom and the response to tier III learners in this section.

Mathematical reasoning/problem solving is to draw four parallelograms and to label the shapes according to the three characteristics. This is problem solving at its best. Students are being asked to apply and analyze a series of steps to re-create each geometric shape by accurately measuring each side and measuring each angle.[13] As students discover that parallelograms are not easy to draw, they will use a ruler to measure each line in relation to each side. This is problem solving and mathematical reasoning. Using the instructional rubric, the candidate can discuss the number of students who successfully completed the assignment.

The candidate is asked to send three student work samples with the assessment materials. These examples should be representative of each tier group. This will give the candidate an opportunity to discuss mathematical errors, confusion, and partial understanding.[14] The candidate is being asked to analyze the student work samples to design a "targeted learning objective" for these students.

This will be the basis for a reengagement lesson. The candidate is being asked to describe the reengagement lesson that the candidate designed to ensure that these students achieve the stated objective from the previous lesson.

In the No Child Left Behind environment, the objective stays the same; the strategy changes. The candidate is asked again to restate the common core standard and to describe the strategies and learning tasks the students will complete, as well as any new resources the candidate may be using.

The candidate is also asked to describe the assessments for informal and formal use during the learning segment. In the example in chapter 2, the candidate used a pop-up math video on the smartboard to reintroduce the concept of shapes. After this video, the candidate redirected the lesson back to the original instructional rubric and continued the lesson using math buddies.

At the end of the lesson, the candidate provided all students with exit slips and asked what they liked about this lesson. The students responded that they enjoyed working with their buddies and they really liked the video.

The candidate is asked to submit three work samples from this lesson. The focus of this response should be on the identified needs of the students in the reengagement lesson. For example, the candidate explained that the students were confused by the words "parallel" and "intersection." The candidate then decided that the students would perform better if they saw an animated video of lines coming together as shapes. When the students were asked to draw the four shapes on their own, 100 percent of the students could then complete the task of drawing and labeling the shapes.

The candidate referred to the exit slips and the students responded that they really enjoyed the pop-up math video. The candidate could write that in future math lessons in geometry, the candidate will use pop-up math videos because they have a visual component to ensure better comprehension of the math concepts for all students.

THINGS TO REMEMBER

- Assessments' most important purpose is not proving instruction but improving instruction.[15]
- Each learning segment is tied to a standard, which is connected to a series of tasks that students must achieve in order to meet the standard. Student progress is linked to the continual assessment of each task during every lesson in every learning segment in every unit. This is the key idea behind the edTPA.
- In task 3, "assessing students' literacy learning," there are four corresponding assessments that each candidate needs to address: the first is the academic assessment of the students; the second is the formative assessment of candidate's videotaped lesson; the third is the formative assessment of student work samples; and the fourth is the summative assessment using exit slips and class work or homework assignments.
- In task 4, "assessing students' mathematics learning," there are four corresponding assessments that the candidate needs to address. The first is an assessment of the whole class or core instruction. The second formative assessment is to identify one area where students struggled mathematically; this should be demonstrated through three student work samples, and the students should represent tier I, II, and III learners. Third is the formative assessment of three student work samples; this is

the summative assessment of the lesson as demonstrated in the exit slips and homework assignment. The fourth is the design of the reengagement lesson for tier II and III students; this assessment is from student work samples and exit slips.

- Formative assessments inform the candidate about what the students know before and during the lesson. Summative assessments are used at the end of the learning segment to make decisions about new instruction. Summative means "summing up" the data.

- Diagnostic assessments are designed to determine what the students know and what they do not know by selecting a particular skill for each question. Alternative and authentic assessments are used to describe an assessment wherein students demonstrate what they have learned in real-life situations. Performance assessments are designed to have the student demonstrate their work. The edTPA is an example of a performance assessment.

- The candidate demonstrates the assessment of student learners in the lesson plan under the discussion of "modifications and adaptations." A formative assessment can be completed as students participate in the core instruction of the lesson by using a rubric.

- The instructional rubric is designed using Bloom's taxonomy. The candidate can use this rubric to explain to the evaluator why the lesson needed to be redirected. Student work samples can be examples of student work used for formative or summative assessments. Candidates completing the exam in 2015 are asked to use an assessment tool and to respond to the students' work.

- The candidate is asked to explain to the evaluator how the instruction engaged students in developing an essential literacy strategy and requisite skills.

- The essential literacy strategy is identified in the standard.

- The requisite skills are the skills that students will practice and use to execute the essential literacy strategy.

- The candidate is asked to divide the summary into patterns of learning. The patterns referred to are (1) conceptual understanding; (2) procedural fluency; (3) mathematical reasoning/problem-solving skills.[16]

- Conceptual understanding refers to the standard.

- Fluency builds on conceptual understanding and strategic reasoning and problem solving, and thus refers to the exploration and discussion of the learning process for all of the students in the core instruction.
- Mathematical reasoning/problem-solving skills refers to the outcome of the instruction: Students are asked to apply and analyze a series of steps to re-create each geometric shape by accurately measuring each side and each angle.
- Stay on the path, answer the questions that are being asked, and refer to all of the rubrics.
- Check your work!

NOTES

1. Cooper, David J., and Nancy D. Kiger. *Literacy Assessment: Helping Teachers Plan Instruction.* 4th ed. Belmont, CA: Wadsworth Cengage Learning, 2011. 12.

2. Stufflebeam, D. L., W. J. Foley, W. J. Gelpert, L. R. Hammond, H. O. Merriman, and M. M. Provus. *Educational Evaluation and Decision Making in Education.* Itasca, IL: Peacock, 1971.

3. Stanford Center for Assessment and Equity. *edTPA Elementary Education Assessment Handbook.* 2013. 31–32.

4. Stanford Center for Assessment and Equity, *edTPA Elementary Education Assessment Handbook*, 41–45.

5. Beirne, Dianna, and Kathleen Velsor. *Engaging Students: Using the Unit in Comprehensive Lesson Planning.* New York: Rowman & Littlefield Education, 2012. 72–74.

6. Kauchak, D., and P. D. Eggen. *Learning and Teaching: Research-Based Methods.* 5th ed. Boston, MA: Allyn and Bacon, 2006.

7. Kauchak and Eggen, *Learning and Teaching: Research-Based Methods.*

8. Stanford Center for Assessment and Equity, *edTPA Elementary Education Assessment Handbook*, 26.

9. Stanford Center for Assessment and Equity, *edTPA Elementary Education Assessment Handbook*, 65.

10. Beirne and Velsor, *Engaging Students*, 25–27.

11. Stanford Center for Assessment and Equity, *edTPA Elementary Education Assessment Handbook*, 65–67.

12. National Council of Teachers of Mathematics and Council of Chief State School Officers, www.nctm.org/Standards-and-Positions/Position-Statements/Procedural-Fluency-in-Mathematics. 2010.

13. Ibid.

14. Stanford Center for Assessment, *edTPA Elementary Education Assessment Handbook*, 44.

15. Stufflebeam et al., *Educational Evaluation and Decision Making in Education*.

16. Stanford Center for Assessment and Equity, *edTPA Elementary Education Assessment Handbook*, 65–67.

6

edTPA Response by Jessica Spero

In the previous chapters, candidates were introduced to the key ideas for completing the edTPA. The first chapter discussed how to determine the nature of the school district and the students in the candidate's class. These are actual prompts and responses to the first set of questions.

ABOUT THE SCHOOL WHERE YOU ARE TEACHING

1. In what type of school do you teach?

   Elementary school: [The elementary school that I teach in includes grades 3 through 5. The district has two primary schools K–2 and three elementary schools with grades 3–5.]
   Middle school: [ ]
   Other (please describe): [ ]

   Urban: [ ]
   Suburban: [The school I am teaching in is in a suburban area on Long Island. This school is included in a high needs district where 51 percent of the population is on the poverty line.]
   Rural: [ ]

2. List any special features of your school or classroom setting (e.g., charter, co-teaching, themed magnet, classroom aide, bilingual, team taught

with a special education teacher) that will affect your teaching in this learning segment.

[The classroom is a co-teaching inclusion setting. This team is taught with one general education and one special education teacher. There are also two aides who assist the three students with generated IEPs. There are six English language learners. The reading teacher pushes in every day during the ELA block to assist all students with primary focus on the English language learners and IEPs. She will be assisting these students when necessary throughout my learning segment but mostly when the students are working independently.]

3. Describe any district, school, or cooperating teacher requirements or expectations that might affect your planning or delivery of instruction, such as required curricula, pacing plan, use of specific instructional strategies, or standardized tests.

[The district requires us to use the common core state standards when instructing in our school. We must teach from the *Journeys* textbook, which runs parallel to the state standards. We are instructed to follow the lesson plan outlines in the teacher's edition of the textbook. The lessons from *Journeys* are our required curricula. These scripted lessons leave very little room for originality because there are set targets to be accomplished for each day of the unit. It is sometimes hard to fit in every anticipated task from each lesson in the unit given the amount of time we have to work with for the ELA block. A lot of time is spent on preparing for schoolwide benchmark testing and state testing exams and can take away from ELA instruction. We have been pressed for time lately with all of the snow days we have had.]

ABOUT THE CLASS FEATURED IN THIS ASSESSMENT

1. How much time is devoted each day to literacy instruction in your classroom?

[Literacy instruction can go from one and a half hours to two hours, depending on whether any lessons need more time to be completed before lunch. Typically phonics, spelling, grammar, or vocabulary is done before moving onto reading or writing, depending on the lesson plans.]

2. Is there any ability grouping or tracking in literacy? If so, please describe how it affects your class.

[The six English language learners and below-reading-level students are consistently tracked in literacy. The reading teacher meets with them for ELA every day and monitors their progress and what they need to work on. This does not negatively affect my class, and if anything it provides additional support for the whole class having a reading teacher available during lessons. Although she focuses on them, she does assist the classroom teacher sometimes in her ELA lessons. When working in their reading groups, students are split into four groups based on their reading levels. For the purpose of my learning segment, students will not be broken into their groups so this will not affect my instruction.]

3. Identify any textbook or instructional program you primarily use for literacy instruction. If a textbook, please provide the title, publisher, and date of publication.

[The textbook and instruction program I used for literacy instruction is *Journeys*. It is a Pearson Textbook, *Journeys* Grade 5, published by Houghton Mifflin Harcourt Publishing Company (2014).]

4. List other resources (e.g., electronic whiteboard, classroom library or other text sets, online professional resources) you use for literacy instruction in this class.

[Typically I use the smartboard for literacy instruction in class. I often display visuals of the textbook pages and assignments on the board so students can follow along. *Journeys* include audio readings of the stories that could be played through the smartboard. If there is ever a technological problem with the smartboard, I use the chalkboard. The classroom teacher also has a library for students to independently read during DEAR (drop everything and read) time. She has books in bins separated by reading levels and also has encyclopedias, dictionaries, and thesauruses.]

ABOUT THE STUDENTS IN THE
CLASS FEATURED IN THIS ASSESSMENT

1. Grade level(s): [5th grade]
2. Number of
   * students in the class [18]
   * males [10] females [8]
3. Complete the chart below to summarize required or needed supports, accommodations, or modifications for your students that will affect your **literacy** instruction in this learning segment. As needed, consult with your cooperating teacher to complete the chart. Some rows have been completed in italics as examples. Use as many rows as you need.

   Consider the variety of learners in your class who may require different strategies/support or accommodations/modification to instruction

Table 6.1. **Students with Specific Learning Needs**

IEP/504 Plans: Classification/Needs	Number of Students	Supports, Accommodations, Modifications, Pertinent IEP Goals
IEP: ADHD	1	Student sits with a good role model, allowed extra time to complete independent tasks, pair written instructions with oral instruction, seek to involve student in the lesson, guided instruction when answering a question, provide short break between assignments, frequently compliment positive behavior and work prompt, read small amounts at a time.
IEP: Below reading level	2	Reading teacher pushes in during ELA block to work with these students. Audio texts and hearing fluent reading helps comprehension. Reading teacher assists them while they are working independently.
English Language Learners	6	Audio text, targeted guided reading, guided questioning, cooperative learning groups with peers, taught new vocabulary in context, allow room for oral assessment, use actions and gestures to explain unfamiliar words.

or assessment (e.g., students with IEPs or 504 plans, English language learners, struggling readers, underperforming students or those with gaps in academic knowledge, and/or gifted students needing greater support or challenge).

LESSON PLAN FOR LITERACY UNIT

Lesson 1

Topic: Introduce Vocabulary
Level: 5th Grade
Estimated Time: 50 minutes
Learning Standards: L.5.4c: Consult reference materials, both print and digital, to find pronunciation and determine or clarify meaning. L.5.6: Acquire and use general academic and domain-specific words and phrases.
Classroom Context: There are eighteen students in the classroom: ten boys and eight girls.
Objectives: Students will be able to acquire and comprehend vocabulary words that will be used throughout the learning segment. Students will be able to work cooperatively in a small group setting.
Behavioral Objectives: [Learning Targets] Students will be able to:

Remembering: Activate prior knowledge to read and comprehend new vocabulary words.
Understanding: Give definitions in their own words.
Applying: Read and explain sentences on the front of the vocabulary cards. Give an example of the vocabulary word in a new sentence.
Analyzing: Complete the "talk it over" activity in cooperative learning groups.
Evaluating: Share their answers with the class and hold a group discussion.

Essential Questions: How can we understand vocabulary words in context?
Procedure:

1. Teacher will direct students to turn to pages 322–23 in their *Journeys* textbook.
2. Teacher will display the ten *Vocabulary in Context* cards in the front of the class on the smartboard for discussion.

3. Teacher will go through each card entirely before moving on to the next. Read and pronounce the vocabulary word once alone and then together as a class. Teacher will explain the word by reading aloud the explanation on the back of the card under "what does it mean?"
4. Discuss vocabulary in context. Ask a student to read the sentence on the front of the card. Re-read it to the class and ask them to explain the sentence. After receiving an accurate explanation, give an example of the vocabulary word in a new sentence. Then ask students to share some of their own examples of using the vocabulary word in a new sentence.
5. Finally, the teacher will discuss the "think about it" question with the students on the back of the card. Repeat steps three through five using the cards for each vocabulary word.
6. Students will then work cooperatively with their tables to complete the "talk it over" activity for fifteen minutes. Each table will receive two cards and each group will submit one piece of loose leaf paper containing the group's answers. Students will share their answers with the class.
7. As an exit slip, students will complete the vocabulary worksheet.

Assessment Plan:
Students will be assessed informally based on the chart in the assessment materials document. The summative assessment will be the group activity "talk it over" and the vocabulary exit slip.

Modifications/Accommodations: For the English language learners, use actions to demonstrate the meanings of words such as embark, surveyed, and cramped. Have students emulate the actions as you say the word. Walk around to each group and ensure students are on the right track and understanding their task activity, "talk it over." Allow IEP student to take frequent breaks if necessary. Reading teacher will rotate around the room to the ELL and struggling readers.

Materials: *Journeys* textbook, *Vocabulary in Context* cards, *Vocabulary in Context* cards visual on the smartboard, pens, loose leaf paper.

Journeys Grade 5, published by Houghton Mifflin Harcourt Publishing Company (2014).

Lesson 2

Topic: Text Evidence, "Dangerous Crossing"
Level: 5th Grade
Estimated Time: 50 minutes
Classroom Context: There are eighteen students in the classroom: ten boys and eight girls.
Learning Standards: R.L. 5.1: Quote accurately from a text when explaining what the text says explicitly and when drawing inferences from the text. R.L. 5.10: Read and comprehend literature.
Objectives: Students will be able to read with a purpose and use text evidence to support their thinking. Students will be able to use context clues to help them understand their vocabulary words in the text.
Learning Targets: Students will be able to:

Remembering: What is historical fiction? What is evidence? Define and discuss vocabulary words from lesson 1 while reading the story.
Understanding: Verbally explain when text evidence is useful.
Applying: Use evidence from the illustrations in the story to visualize and make inferences.
Analyzing: Find evidence from the text to support answers for "thinking through the text" questions.
Evaluating: Verbally summarize parts of the story.

Essential Questions: How can we use text evidence to support our inferences and answers?
Procedure:

1. Teacher will begin the lesson by having the students turn to the story "Dangerous Crossing" in their *Journeys* textbooks and vocabulary sheets. Teacher will ask the students to recall "Mother and Son," the historical fiction piece we have previously read. Teacher will give a quick summary of "Mother and Son."
2. Teacher will ask students to define the elements of historical fiction in their own words and introduce them to another historical fiction story called "Dangerous Crossing."

3. Teacher will go over text evidence before beginning the story. T: What is the definition of text evidence? T: When do we use text evidence? T: How is text evidence helpful?
4. Begin the audio for the story "Dangerous Crossing." Teacher will stop and discuss the vocabulary words in the text. Teacher will help students use context clues to figure out alternate meanings of vocabulary words.
5. Throughout the story, teacher will ask students to make inferences based on the illustrations. T: What is happening in this illustration? T: What inferences can we make?
6. Teacher will ask students to visualize characters' feelings throughout the story based on details and evidence from the text. T: How do you think Johnny felt when . . . ?"
7. After completing the audio of "Dangerous Crossing," teacher will summarize with the students the important events that happened in the story. Teacher will help guide the discussion ensuring that students are paying attention to sequence. Students will be asked to copy any definitions from the board onto their vocabulary sheets.
8. Teacher will hand out "thinking through the text" questions to work on independently for about twenty minutes. Students should go back to the appropriate pages to look for text evidence to support their answers. When they are all completed, students will be asked to share answers for each of the eight questions.
9. To conclude the lesson, students will be given a sheet of paper for an exit slip. The exit slip will say, "Answer in complete sentences: What did we learn today about text evidence? What is the definition of text evidence? When do we use text evidence? Why do we use text evidence?"

Assessment Plan:
Students will be formally assessed based on the charts in the assessment materials document. The summative assessment will be the completion of the "thinking through the text" questions. Students must complete all eight questions by the end of the period. Teacher will collect the questions and exit slips to check for understanding.

Modifications/Adaptations: Teacher will play the audio of the story "Dangerous Crossing" for the English language learners who comprehend better when listening and following along with the text. Stopping the audio to have a class discussion throughout the story also helps the IEP student with ADHD to stay on task and to not lose interest in the story. Allow IEP student to take frequent breaks if necessary. Students will have their vocabulary word list in front of them for the English language learners so that they can refer back to words they don't know. Teacher will provide students with page numbers to focus on to guide them in the right direction when answering the "thinking through the text" questions.

Materials: *Journeys* Textbook with the story "Dangerous Crossing," vocabulary word list, "thinking through the text" questions, smartboard, chalkboard.

Journeys Grade 5, published by Houghton Mifflin Harcourt Publishing Company (2014).

Lesson 3

Topic: Understanding Cause and Effect
Level: 5th Grade
Estimated Time: 45–50 minutes
Classroom Context: There are eighteen students in the classroom: ten boys and eight girls.
Learning Standards: R.L. 5.5: Explain how chapters, scenes, or stanzas fit together to provide overall structure. R.I. 5.5: Compare and contrast the overall structure (e.g., chronology, comparison, cause/effect, problem/solution) of events, ideas, concepts, or information.
Objectives: Students will be able to recognize cause and effect relationships. Students will complete a graph organizer to demonstrate how the author displays cause and effect relationships in the text.
Essential Questions: How can we identify cause and effect in historical fiction?
Behavioral Objectives/ Learning Targets:

Remembering: What is cause and effect? Ability to define it.
Understanding: Ability to explain what cause and effect is.
Applying: Use of examples to show a cause and effect relationship.
Analyzing: After viewing the PowerPoint presentation, students should be able to differentiate between the cause and the effect from each slide.
Evaluating: Find examples of cause and effect relationships from the text.

Procedure:

1. Teacher will explain to students that good readers read with a purpose and should ask themselves why events happen in a story. To introduce the lesson, teacher will explain to students that one event leads to another and these events contribute to the action of the story.

2. Teacher will ask students to define cause and effect. As a class we will agree on a definition. Students will copy these terms in their reading notebooks. T: Cause is what makes something happen, while the effect is reaction to what happened.

3. Teacher will ask students to give and explain their own examples of cause and effect. Give the students an example of a cause and effect relationship, such as: Mark didn't study on his test, therefore he got a 38 percent on his test. Write it on the board. T: Which is the cause? Which is the effect?

4. Teacher will explain to the students that there are clue words in the text that can signal a cause and effect relationship. Ask the students if they know which word in the sentence is the clue word (therefore). Circle "therefore" on the board. Brainstorm and list other clue words as a class, such as: therefore, due to, as a result, consequently, since, nevertheless, so that, because, this/that is how, for this/that reason, thus, if . . . then. Teacher will write these words on a chart and students will copy it in their notebooks.

5. Teacher will then play a short PowerPoint presentation for the class, which includes definitions of cause and effect. It also gives a couple examples of cause and effect relationships in which students need to decide what sentence is the cause and what is the effect.

6. Students will listen to the audio of "Dangerous Crossing" for the second time. Teacher will hand each child a few Post-It notes. Teacher will ask the students to make note of any cause and effect relationship they hear throughout the story. Encourage students to listen for clue words to help them stay on task.

7. Throughout the story, teacher will summarize when necessary in order to make the connection between the story and the American Revolution. Students have been previously exposed to the American Revolution throughout the year.

8. After listening to the story, students will work cooperatively with their tables, filling out the cause and effect worksheet. They will use their notes and focus on pages 330–31, 334–35, and 339. Details and direct quotes from the story should be used. There should be at least three cause and effect relationships on their charts. They will be given about fifteen minutes to complete this task.

9. After completing the cause and effect graphic organizer, students will be asked to share their findings with the class. Students should copy any cause and effect relationships they didn't find and their corresponding page numbers.

10. Exit slip: "Choose a cause and effect example from 'Dangerous Crossing' that you used in your graphic organizer. Write a short paragraph explaining how the character felt before the event happened and after the event happened. Use details and quotes from the text to support your answer."

Assessment Plan: Students will be assessed formatively based on the chart listed in the assessment materials document. The summative assessment will be the cause and effect graphic organizers. It will be checked to ensure students were able to accurately pull cause and effect relationships from the text. Another summative assessment will be the exit slip paragraph.

Modifications/Adaptions: Teacher will use the PowerPoint presentation to show multiple examples of cause and effect relationships to guide the English language learners. Students will work cooperatively with their tables in order to promote better understanding of how to find cause and effect relationships in the text. The list of clue words will remain on the board for students to refer to. Allow IEP student to take frequent breaks if necessary. Students that finish early will be asked to write three other examples of cause and effect relationships in their reading notebooks.

Materials: *Journeys* textbook with story "Dangerous Crossing," cause and effect graphic organizer, smartboard, cause and effect PowerPoint presentation, student reading notebooks, chart paper, pencils, markers.

Journeys Grade 5, published by Houghton Mifflin Harcourt Publishing Company (2014).

ASSESSMENTS

[The candidate is required to attach a copy of the student assignments and the assessment rubrics.]

Thinking through the Text

"Dangerous Crossing" Text-Based Evidence

Directions: Use the information from the text to support your thinking.

1. Based on the statement "the blustering snow stung his cheek like nettles," what do you think nettles are? (p. 328)

2. What do you learn about John Adams from his willingness to go on a sea voyage in midwinter? (p. 329)

3. What does the phrase "bowing to their enthusiasm" mean? What action on Captain Tucker's part provides a context clue to help you understand the phrase as it is used in the text? (p. 332)

4. Based on the narrator's description of Johnny's thoughts, how did he feel about being in a possible battle? How do you know? (p. 333)

5. How does the diary quotation contribute to the story? (p. 333)

6. Quote the text details that help you visualize Johnny's experience with the storm. (p. 334)

7. What evidence does the author provide to support the idea that John Adams wasn't extremely bothered by this event? (p. 335)

8. What text evidence does the author provide to show how John Adams felt about finally reaching France? (p. 339)

Figure 6.1. Literacy Worksheet
Source: Jessica Spero

Date: 2/11/14

Thinking through the Text

"Dangerous Crossing" Text-Based Evidence

Directions: Use the information from the text to support your thinking.

1. Based on the statement "the blustering snow stung his cheek like nettles," what do you think nettles are? (p. 328)

Nettles can be something sharp or irritating because they can cause a stinging sensation.

2. What do you learn about John Adams from his willingness to go on a sea voyage in midwinter? (p. 329)

I learned about John Adams of his willingness is brave because it was a hard task.

3. What does the phrase "bowing to their enthusiasm" mean? What action on Captain Tucker's part provides a context clue to help you understand the phrase as it is used in the text? (p. 332)

The Captain Tucker agree the Boston to see the other ships.

4. Based on the narrator's description of Johnny's thoughts, how did he feel about being in a possible battle? How do you know? (p. 333)

Johnny is excited. He compared watching in earlier battle to being "in the thick of things".

5. How does the diary quotation contribute to the story? (p. 333)

The diary quotation lets us hear John's voice describing the events.

6. Quote the text details that help you visualize Johnny's experience with the storm. (p. 334)

Johnny's experience with the storm is scared because it said "soon the ship began to pitch, rocking violently back and forth".

7. What evidence does the author provide to support the idea that John Adams wasn't extremely bothered by this event? (p. 335)

The quotes in this diary were based on facts not feeling. This shows he was able to stay calm.

8. What text evidence does the author provide to show how John Adams felt about finally reaching France? (p. 339)

John Adams felt proud about finally reaching France because it said "The pleasure resulting from the sight of Land, Cattle, House, etc. after so long and dangerous voyage is very great".

Figure 6.2. Student Literacy Work Samples
Source: Jessica Spero

Thinking through the Text

"Dangerous Crossing" Text-Based Evidence

Directions: Use the information from the text to support your thinking.

1. Based on the statement "the blustering snow stung his cheek like nettles," what do you think nettles are? (p. 328)

Nettles can be something sharp or irratang because heavy set stingy sentgticy

2. What do you learn about John Adams from his willingness to go on a sea voyage in midwinter? (p. 329)

Amid winter voyage was dangerous so you know John adams is brave

3. What does the phrase "bowing to their enthusiasm mean? What action on Captain Tucker's part provides a context clue to help you understand the phrase as it is used in the text? (p. 332)

bowing to their enthusiasm means to agree when you give up! Like when captain tucker agreed with the soiders

4. Based on the narrator's description of Johnny's thoughts, how did he feel about being in a possible battle? How do you know? (p. 333)

Johnny is excited. He compared being in another battle to being in the thick of things

5. How does the diary quotation contribute to the story? (p. 333)

The diary quotations lets us hear Johns voiced feeling the event

6. Quote the text details that help you visualize Johnny's experience with the storm. (p. 334)

It was with utmost difficult. C the ship has been struck with lightning Johnny is scared

7. What evidence does the author provide to support the idea that John Adams wasn't extremely bothered by this event? (p. 335)

The quote in his diary is on facts not feelings this shows the he was able to stay calm

8. What text evidence does the author provide to show how John Adams felt about finally reaching France? (p. 339)

John felt happy about reaching France. You know this because it says "The pleasure resulting from sight of land, cattle, Horses and etc. After 8 long and dangerous a voyage is very great".

Figure 6.3. Student Literacy Work Samples
Source: Jessica Spero

Date: <u>2/11</u>

Thinking through the Text

"Dangerous Crossing" Text-Based Evidence

Directions: Use the information from the text to support your thinking.

1. Based on the statement "the blustering snow stung his cheek like nettles," what do you think nettles are? (p. 328)

Nettles can be sharp and irritating

2. What do you learn about John Adams from his willingness to go on a sea voyage in midwinter? (p. 329)

It was very dangerise for them to cross the sea.

3. What does the phrase "bowing to their enthusiasm mean? What action on Captain Tucker's part provides a context clue to help you understand the phrase as it is used in the text? (p. 332)

The captain agree to let Booston to see the ships.

4. Based on the narrator's description of Johnny's thoughts, how did he feel about being in a possible battle? How do you know? (p. 333)

Johny is feeling very excited because he is in a battle.

5. How does the diary quotation contribute to the story? (p. 333)

The diary quotation is telling that a battle is beginning.

6. Quote the text details that help you visualize Johnny's experience with the storm. (p. 334)

" The ship was stroke by lightening and Johny was scared.

7. What evidence does the author provide to support the idea that John Adams wasn't extremely bothered by this event? (p. 335)

Johnys diary is telling that he was happy that his father was calm.

8. What text evidence does the author provide to show how John Adams felt about finally reaching France? (p. 339)

John Adams was happy to make it to france because he said "The pleasure from so long crossing the sea."

Figure 6.4.   Student Literacy Work Samples
Source: Jessica Spero

Learning Targets Core Instruction	Target 3	Acceptable 2	Unacceptable 1	Score
Defining historical fiction and evidence.	Defines both historical fiction and evidence.	Defines only one of the two terms, historical fiction or evidence	Unable to define historical fiction or evidence.	
Defining and discussing vocabulary words throughout the story.	Accurately defines and discusses ten vocabulary words while reading the story.	Accurately defines and discusses at least seven vocabulary words while reading the story.	Accurately defines and discusses fewer than seven vocabulary words while reading the story.	
Verbally explains when text evidence is useful.	Verbally explains when text evidence is useful.	Verbally explains when text evidence is useful with some guidance.	Unable to explain when text evidence is useful.	
Visualize and make inferences based on illustrations.	At least two students accurately visualize and verbally make inferences from the illustrations.	At least one student accurately visualizes and verbally makes an inference from the illustrations.	Does not make the connection between the inferences and the illustrations.	
Finding evidence from the text to support answers.	Finds evidence to accurately complete six of eight "thinking through the text" questions.	Finds evidence to accurately complete five of eight "thinking through the text" questions.	Does not accurately complete at least five "thinking through the text" questions.	
Group discussion to summarize the story.	Actively participates in discussion.	Contributes somewhat to discussion.	Does not contribute to discussion.	

Figure 6.5.   Student Literacy Assessment Rubric
Source: Jessica Spero

Target Journey's Worksheet 3	Acceptable 2	Unacceptable 1	Score
Accurately quotes evidence from the text when asked to support answers in "thinking through the text."	Somewhat quotes from the text when asked to support answers in "thinking through the text."	Unable to quote direct evidence from the text to support answers in "thinking through the text."	
Clearly answers all parts of the problem when the problem asks more than one question.	Somewhat answers all parts of the problem when the problem asks more than one question.	Unable to answer all parts of the problem when the problem asks more than one question.	
Shows clear comprehension of the events that happened in the story.	Somewhat comprehends the events that happened in the story.	Does not comprehend what is going on in the story.	
Answers six out of eight questions correctly.	Answers five out of eight questions correctly.	Does not answer more than five questions correctly.	

Figure 6.6.   Student Literacy Assessment Rubric
Source: Jessica Spero

Central Focus:		State-Adopted Content Standards (or common core state standards, if applicable):	
[The central focuses of these lessons are to build on division skills using one- and two-digit divisors and understand the importance of the relationship between multiplication and division.]		[CC.5.NBT.6: Find whole-number quotients of whole numbers with up to four-digit dividends and two-digit divisors, using strategies based on place value, the properties of operations, and/or the relationship between multiplication and division. CC.5.NBT.6: Perform operations with multi-digit whole numbers.]	

	Learning Objectives	Instructional Strategies and Learning Tasks	Formative and Summative Assessments
Lesson 1	[Students will be able to divide by two-digit divisors. Students will be able to estimate quotients before solving. Students will be able to check their quotient by using multiplication.]	[Teacher will review vocabulary necessary for division (dividend, divisor, quotient, remainder, and estimate).Teacher will ask students to recall the steps of division they used when dividing with a one-digit divisor. (1) Dad: divide; (2) Mom: multiply; (3) Sister: subtract; (4) Brother: bring down; (5) Rover: repeat or remainder. After teacher does an example, students will be asked to estimate the dividend and divisor to get an estimated quotient before solving in their workbooks. Step 1: use the estimate to place the first digit in the quotient. Step 2: divide the tens. Step 3: divide the ones. Step 4: check your answer. Encourage students to underline what they are trying to find and circle the numbers they need to use.]	[Formative assessment: Students will solve examples on the board and explain the steps they took in order to get to the quotient. Students will work independently in Go Math lesson books after they complete the example with the teacher. Teacher will go over answers with the class at the end of the period. Summative assessment: For homework students will complete a page of the even-numbered problems and show work examples. They will be collected and reviewed to ensure understanding. Target: 8/8; Acceptable: 7/8; Unacceptable: fewer than 7.]
Lesson 2	[Students will play a game while continuing to hone their division skills.	[Reengaging division: Teacher will play "bingo" using division problems. Students will use numbers between 1 and 25 as	Formative assessment: Teacher will go over a few division examples with a two-digit divisor

Figure 6.7. Math Overview
Source: Jessica Spero

	Students will be able to understand the process of finding a quotient with one- and two-digit divisors.]	their quotients for the board. Students will work independently to solve the problems and will cross off the quotient if it is on their board. After five students cross five quotients off their boards vertically, horizontally, or diagonally, the game is complete. Teacher will wrap up the lesson by using division flash cards. Students will be able to use their scrap paper BUT these problems are meant to be answered rapidly.]	on the board. Students will explain the steps and follow along. Summative assessment: At the end of the lesson, students will complete an exit slip worksheet to show understanding of the overall division process. Students are to pick one example and write out the steps they took in order to solve. Target: 9/9; Acceptable: 8/9, Unacceptable: fewer than 8.
Lesson 3	[Students will understand the importance of knowing multiplication when dividing with one- or two-digit divisors. Students will collaborate with each other in a small group setting.]	[Reengagement: Small group for children who struggled with multiplying when dividing. Prior to this lesson, the six struggling students were assigned to practice specific multiplication table flash cards. Teacher will play a multiplication game with students to make practicing more enjoyable. Problems will be completed in their notebooks.]	[Formative assessment: Teacher will review and reengage students in this small group setting. Teacher will go over previous lessons and stress the importance of multiplication in the division process. Summative assessment: For homework ten multiplication problems.]

Figure 6.7. (*continued*)

MATH OVERVIEW

Learning Segment Overview Directions: Briefly describe the instruction preceding the assessment by typing within the brackets in each section of the chart below (no more than two single-spaced pages). Do not delete or alter the chart, both the chart and your description are included in the total page count allowed. Refer to the evidence chart in the handbook to ensure that this document complies with all format specifications. Pages exceeding the maximum will not be scored.

Candidates are required to send actual work samples and demonstrate feedback to the students. These are copies of the actual work samples for both literacy and the math overview. As of fall 2014 candidates are required to discuss the data generated from the scoring rubrics.

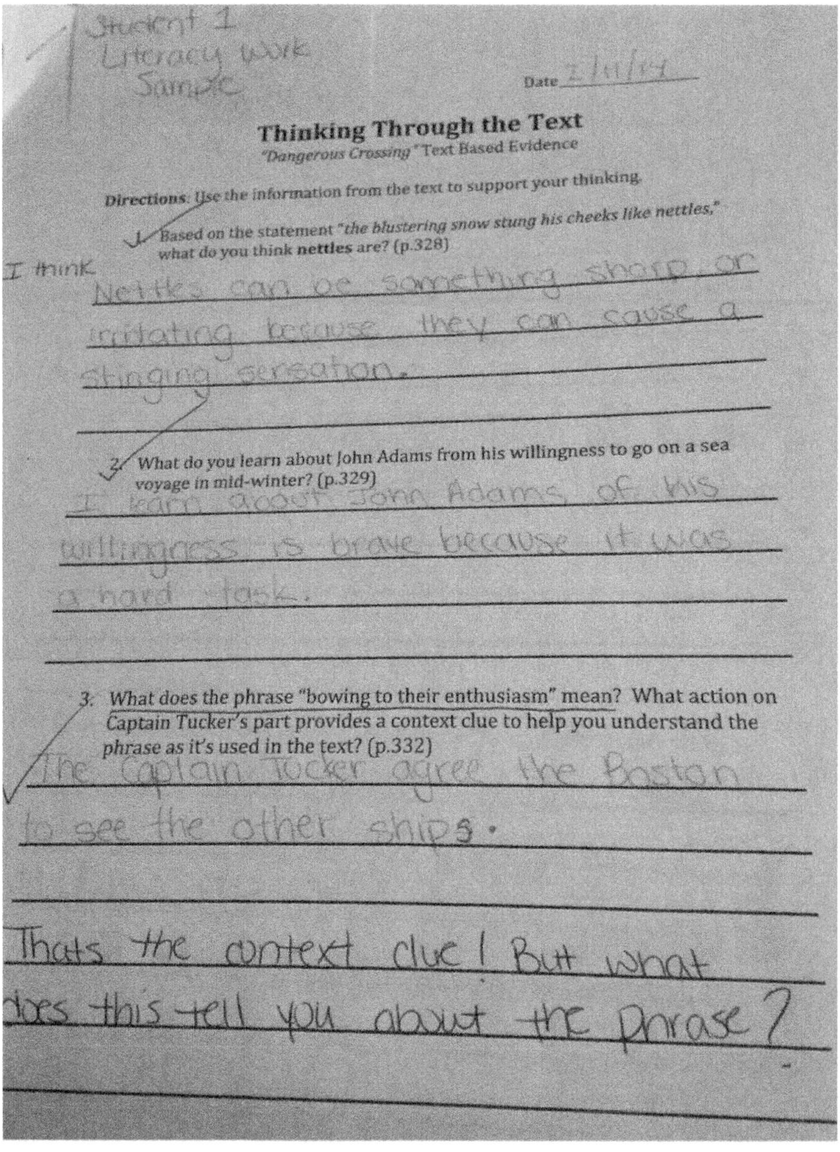

Student 1
Literacy Work
Sample

Date 2/11/14

Thinking Through the Text

"Dangerous Crossing" Text Based Evidence

Directions: Use the information from the text to support your thinking.

1. Based on the statement *"the blustering snow stung his cheeks like nettles,"* what do you think **nettles** are? (p.328)

I think Nettles can be something sharp or irritating because they can cause a stinging sensation.

2. What do you learn about John Adams from his willingness to go on a sea voyage in mid-winter? (p.329)

I learn about John Adams of his willingness is brave because it was a hard task.

3. *What does the phrase "bowing to their enthusiasm" mean? What action on Captain Tucker's part provides a context clue to help you understand the phrase as it's used in the text? (p.332)*

The Captain Tucker agree the Boston to see the other ships.

Thats the context clue! But what does this tell you about the phrase?

Figure 6.8. Student Feedback Literacy

Source: Jessica Spero

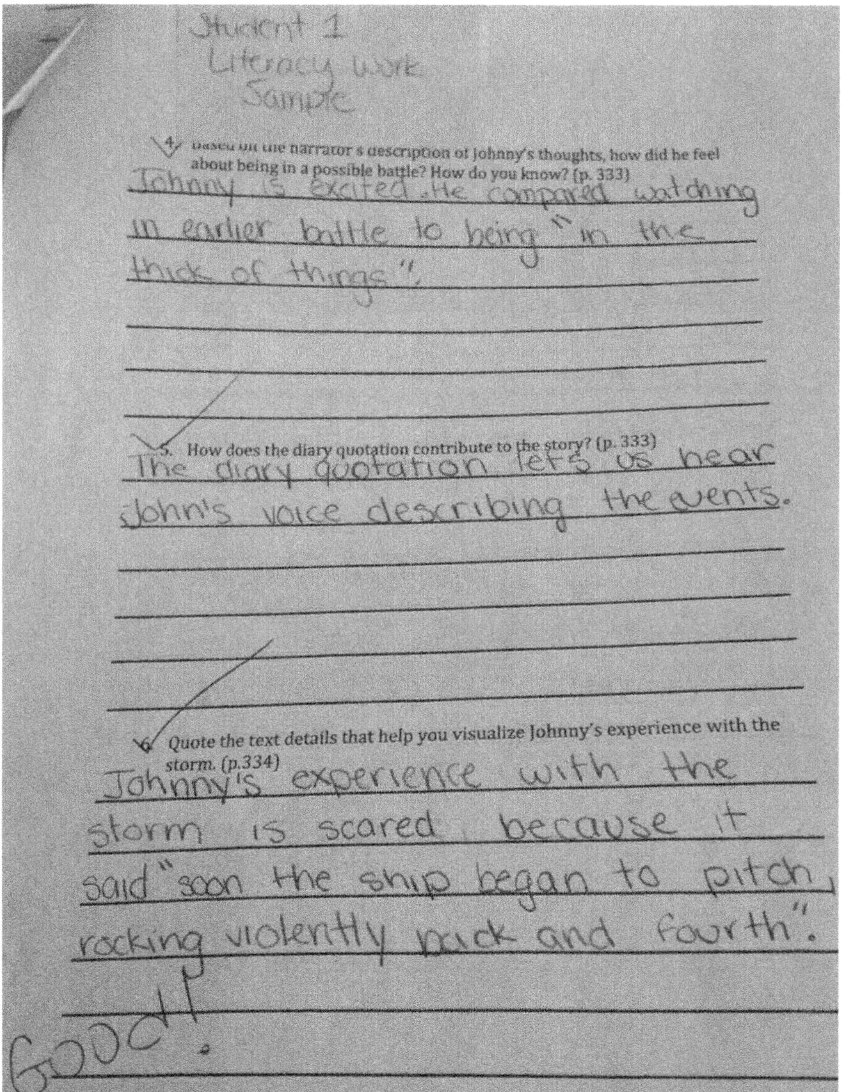

Student 1
Literacy Work
Sample

4. Based on the narrator's description of Johnny's thoughts, how did he feel about being in a possible battle? How do you know? (p. 333)

Johnny is excited. He compared watching in earlier battle to being "in the thick of things".

5. How does the diary quotation contribute to the story? (p. 333)

The diary quotation lets us hear John's voice describing the events.

6. Quote the text details that help you visualize Johnny's experience with the storm. (p.334)

Johnny's experience with the storm is scared because it said "soon the ship began to pitch, rocking violently back and fourth".

Good!

Figure 6.9. Student Feedback Literacy
Source: Jessica Spero

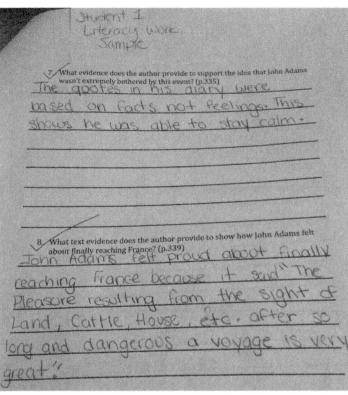

7. What evidence does the author provide to support the idea that John Adams wasn't extremely bothered by this event? (p.335)

The quotes in his diary were based on facts not feelings. This shows he was able to stay calm.

8. What text evidence does the author provide to show how John Adams felt about finally reaching France? (p.339)

John Adams felt proud about finally reaching France because it said "The Pleasure resulting from the sight of Land, Cattle, House, etc. after so long and dangerous a voyage is very great."

Figure 6.10.   Student Feedback Literacy
Source: Jessica Spero

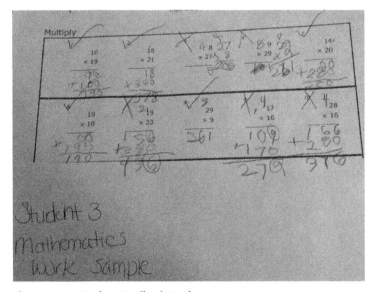

Figure 6.11.   Student Feedback Math
Source: Jessica Spero

THINGS TO REMEMBER

- This is a copy of an actual response to the edTPA from the 2014. In chapter 5, the new requirements have been added. Always refer to the scoring rubric.
- When completing this exam, the candidate allowed at least forty hours to complete all of the sections.
- List all of the schools in the district.
- List all of the special teachers and instructors in the classroom. Be honest about the instructional program in the school. Discuss and footnote the required text or written curriculum. List any limitations such as snow days and test prep. Make it real.
- Describe the nature of the learners in the classroom. Use academic language to support the descriptions of the reading levels and other English language learner students who will be in the learning segment that is used in the video.
- Describe the reading text that is used in the classroom and use APA style to reference the text. Mention all of the technology in the classroom and if it does not work properly all of the time, mention that in case it does not work in the video. Mention all of the literacy activities in the classroom.
- Fill in the chart listing the number of students in each category and ask the cooperating teacher for assistance concerning the best strategies to help each student. Check IEPs if possible.
- Use the lesson plan format outlined in chapter 3. Make sure you identify all of the Bloom's levels in sequence. Make sure they are consistent with the required academic language and use it correctly in your lesson plan. Check for spelling and grammar. Keep the lesson plan less than four pages.
- The candidate should select the second or third lesson in the learning segment. The candidate can discuss the results of the assessments in the previous lesson and how these helped to design the next lesson. Attach student work samples from the lesson shown in the video. The candidate needs to have a rubric for the instructional lesson and a separate rubric for the student work samples. The standard for the lesson should appear in the upper lefthand corner of the rubric. This is what you are measuring.

- Fill in the math overview chart. Lesson 1 is the core instruction. Design the lesson plan using Bloom's taxonomy. Simplify the list using the steps taken. Lesson 2 and 3 are reengagement lessons based on the data from the first lesson. Discuss the use of formative and summative assessments using the rubric and data. Keep to the limited number of pages. Attach three student work samples and discuss results using the data from the scoring rubric.
- The literacy segment and the math segment must be in the same room.
- Good luck!

Appendix A

Bloom's Higher Order Thinking Skills	Verbs	Products
Remembering: students express and recall information	list, memorize, review, define, name, match, retrieve, recognize, recall	label, list, definition, test, reproduction, recitation, tape
Understanding: students construct meaning from oral, graphic, or written messages	explain, summarize, generalize, interpret, infer, paraphrase, classify	report, illustration, matching chart, demonstration, dramatization
Applying: students use new information across contexts, executing and implementing a procedure	apply, construct, demonstrate, solve, show, translate, illustrate	diagram, model, report, lesson, photograph, collection, map, puzzle, diary
Analyzing: students break material into constituent parts, determining how the parts relate to the whole	analyze, distinguish, differentiate, classify, contrast, compare, order	diagram, questionnaire, graph, outline, survey, report, chart, conclusion
Evaluating: students make judgments based on criteria and standards through checking and critique	integrate, compose, formulate, modify, hypothesize, create, invent	plan, formulate, invention, design, poem, solution, art media/prediction story, advertisement
Creating: students put elements together into a coherent, functional whole or reorganize into a new pattern or structure	judge, decide, evaluate, verify, criticize, defend, select, justify, assess	editorial, debate, scale, verdict, value, recommendation, conclusion, report, opinion

Bloom's Higher Order Thinking Skills

Appendix B

Name:
Topic:
Level:
Estimated Time: 35–45 minutes
Classroom Context:
Learning Standards:
Learning Objective:
Learning Tasks:
• *Remembering*
• *Understanding*
• *Applying*
• *Analyzing*
• *Evaluating*
Procedures:
• Hook (a question)
• I show you/you show me
• Student work sample
• Sharing work samples
• Exit slips
Instructional Strategies:
Modifications/Adaptations:
Assessment Plan:
Materials:
References:

Lesson Plan Format

Glossary of Academic Language

Academic language: The language of the discipline; the vocabulary, language function, syntax, and discourse. The language of literacy and math are in the selected standard and should be used in the learning segment. Candidates need to use these terms during the filming of the learning segment.

ACCESS: Assessing Comprehension and Communication in English for English Language Learners. Levels: 1 entering; 2 beginning; 3 developing; 4 expanding; 5 bridging; 6 reacting.

Artifacts: Real work samples that are completed by students.

Assessment: Ongoing, systematic way of acquiring information about student learning in the classroom.

Bloom's Taxonomy of Higher Order Thinking Skills: Six cognitive levels of thinking that can assist candidates in constructing learning segment targets, tasks, and assessments.

Conceptual understanding: Refers to the common core math standard.

Core instruction: Instruction given to the whole class.

Dual-language: Two languages spoken in one classroom. Students are expected to be literate in both languages. Also called bilingual programs.

ELL: English language learners.

Essential literacy strategy: Identified in the English language common core literacy standard.

Five levels of literacy: Early emergent literacy, emergent literacy, beginning reading and writing, almost fluent reading and writing, fluent reading and writing.

Formative assessments: Designed to inform the candidate about instruction, they can be formal work samples or informal discussions. They should be the same as the stated tasks.

IRA: International Reading Association.

Learning segment: A unit of study consisting of three or more lessons.

Mathematical reasoning/problem-solving skills: The outcome of the instruction when students are asked to apply and analyze a series of mathematical steps.

Mini-lesson: A short lesson used by candidates to redirect the learner back to the learning task.

NYSESLAT: New York State English as a Second Language Test; an exam used to assess a student's fluency in English as a second language.

Patterns of learning: The patterns that the edTPA is referring to are: (1) conceptual understanding; (2) procedural fluency; (3) mathematical reasoning/problem-solving skills.

Procedural fluency: Builds on conceptual understanding and strategic reasoning and problem solving, and thus refers to the exploration and discussion of the learning process for all of the students in the core instruction.

RTI: Response to intervention. School districts are responsible for designing a multi-tier approach to reading assessments for all students in general and special education.

Reengagement lesson: When students do not perform well in a learning segment, the candidate may need to design a reengagement lesson to achieve the desired outcome.

Requisite literacy skills: The skills that students practice and use to execute the essential literacy strategy.

Rubric: Used as an assessment or evaluation tool to assess student learning. Rubrics should match the stated tasks.

Strategy: A teaching method used to enhance student learning.

Summative assessment: Sums up the learning segment. Class assignments or exit slips can be used to collect data about student learning. In math, a unit test or culminating project in a unit can also be used.

Tasks: A term used by the edTPA to identify learning outcomes needed to complete a literacy or math learning segment.

Tier I: Students who are in the core instruction and need a mini-lesson or a different strategy to complete the learning tasks.

Tier II: Students who are in the core instruction and need a separate learning segment to complete the task; this could be a reengagement lesson.

Tier III: Students who are in the core instruction and have been identified to have special learning modifications.

Index

CPSIA information can be obtained at www.ICGtesting.com
Printed in the USA
BVOW08s1140040815

411697BV00001B/3/P